CONTENTS

Here are eight plays by writers aged ten to eighteen, selected from the winners of the 1983 and 1984 Young Playwrights Festivals. Each of these plays was given a professional production at a New York theater.

These extraordinary plays cover an astonishing range of subjects: family, friendship, love, loneliness, divorce, blind dates, even the future of the human race. Some are hilarious, one is truly macabre, and some are deeply moving. The Festival is open to nearly any kind of play. If you're under nineteen, why not write one and enter? Read on, and you'll find out how.

"This is a wonderful idea for young people, and a very generous one from old dramatists."
—Clive Barnes, *New York Post*

"While the new authors learn about the theater, audiences learn what's on their minds and discover how skillfully they put their ideas on the stage. From either side, it's a rewarding experience."   —Allan Wallach, *Newsday*

"One hopes that the writers never learn to stop taking the chances that enliven their plays. Unencumbered by theatrical 'rules' and fashions, the young playwrights assume that anything is possible and write honestly and spontaneously. Let's pray that they never grow up."
—Frank Rich, *The New York Times*

WENDY LAMB is a consulting editor of books for young readers at Delacorte Press. Her short stories and articles have appeared in several magazines.

The eight plays in this anthology were selected from seventeen plays given full productions or staged readings in the Young Playwrights Festival in 1983 and 1984. Produced by the Foundation of the Dramatists Guild, the Festival seeks to identify and encourage talented playwrights under the age of nineteen. The 1983 Festival was presented at Circle Repertory Company and the 1984 Festival at the New York Shakespeare Festival's Public Theater in New York City. Information about the Young Playwrights Festival is available at the Foundation of the Dramatists Guild, 234 West 44th Street, New York, New York 10036.

YOUNG PLAYWRIGHTS FESTIVAL STAFF

Peggy C. Hansen, Producing Director
Gerald Chapman, Education Director
Sheri Goldhirsch, Associate Director
Richard Wolcott, Administrative Assistant

YOUNG PLAYWRIGHTS FESTIVAL COMMITTEE

Stephen Sondheim, Chairman
Christopher Durang
Jules Feiffer
Charles Fuller
Ruth Goetz
Micki Grant
A. R. Gurney
Murray Horwitz
David E. LeVine
Eve Merriam
Mary Rodgers

The Young Playwrights Festival is supported by numerous foundations, corporations, and individuals. In 1983 and 1984 major funding was provided by the Exxon Corporation, as well as by the Axe-Houghton Foundation, the Barker Welfare Foundation, the Charles Ulrick and Josephine Bay Foundation, CBS Inc., the Jean and Louis Dreyfus Foundation, the Herman Goldman Foundation, the Exxon Education Foundation, the League of New York Theatres and Producers, the George Link, Jr., Foundation, the David Merrick Arts Foundation, the Metropolitan Life Foundation, the Harold and Beatrice Renfield Foundation, the Richard and Dorothy Rodgers Foundation, and the Shubert Foundation. The Festival is made possible in part with funds from the New York State Council on the Arts. To all of the above and to our many other contributors, the Festival extends grateful appreciation.

From the 1983 and 1984
Young Playwrights
Festival

MEETING THE WINTER BIKE RIDER And Other Prize-Winning Plays

Edited by Wendy Lamb
Introduction by Gerald Chapman

Published by
Dell Publishing Co., Inc.
1 Dag Hammarskjold Plaza
New York, New York 10017

PHOTO CREDITS:

Front cover:
Jeffrey Marcus, as Mark, and Corey Parker, as Tony, in *Meeting the Winter Bike Rider*,
performed at the Public Theater, New York City, May 1984.
Copyright © 1984 by Martha Swope.

Back cover:
Richard Colman, Copyright © 1985 by Carla Adrian Gahr; Charlie Schulman,
Copyright © 1985 by Martha Swope Associates, Susan Cook; Jason Brown, Patricia Durkin,
Peter Getty, Juan Nunez, Joseph Yesutis.
Copyright © 1983 by Beryl Towbin.

THE BIRTHDAY PRESENT Copyright © 1986 by Charlie Schulman
LIARS Copyright © 1986 by Joseph Yesutis
TENDER PLACES Copyright © 1986 by Jason Brown
A NEW APPROACH TO HUMAN SACRIFICE Copyright © 1986 by Peter Getty
MEETING THE WINTER BIKE RIDER Copyright © 1986 by Juan Nunez
SCRAPS Copyright © 1986 by Tagore J. McIntyre
FIXED UP Copyright © 1986 by Patricia Durkin
THIRD STREET Copyright © 1986 Richard Colman

Introduction Copyright © 1986 by Gerald Chapman

Laurel-Leaf Library® TM 766734, Dell Publishing Co., Inc.
ISBN: 0-440-95548-3
RL: 6.4

Printed in the United States of America
April 1986
10 9 8 7 6 5 4 3 2 1

WFH

INTRODUCTION by Gerald Chapman

The Young Playwrights Festival

The eight plays in this book are all by people who were aged eighteen or under when they wrote their plays and were therefore eligible to enter an annual play-writing contest called the Young Playwrights Festival. The Festival occurs annually, usually in the spring, and it consists of professional productions of the winning scripts in a major off-Broadway theater. The young authors travel to New York from all over the United States (all expenses paid!) and share in the excitement and hard work of putting on their plays.

The Young Playwrights Festival has become such a popular tradition, with offshoots springing up in regional theaters all over the United States, that it is easy to forget how strange and innovative it was at the beginning. In England I used to run a similar venture at London's famous Royal Court Theatre.

In 1980 Stephen Sondheim, the celebrated composer and lyricist, and president of the Dramatists Guild at the time, happened to be in London and saw the Royal Court project. He invited me to New York to establish the American Festival, and in 1982 ten plays by writers aged eight to eighteen opened at Circle Repertory Company. Never before in this country had the work of a child or a teenager been staged with such professional theatrical expertise. In 1983 (at Circle Rep) and 1984 (at the New York Shakespeare Festival's Public Theater) the eight plays you have in your hand were also produced with total professionalism. Each year the tradition continues to grow. And for the young playwrights themselves, each year offers a series of unusual challenges.

Writing the Play

The first challenge is actually deciding to write a play at all. Some of the winners wrote their plays by themselves, without any guidance or advice; others worked on them as class assignments or in a workshop. Three of the writers in this book, Peter Getty, Charlie Schulman, and Joseph Yesutis, were required to write a play as part of their language arts curriculum. This experience helped them a great deal in the long run. By testing the play out (in a reading or in performance) before their class, they knew more clearly where to make revisions. A fourth writer, Richard Colman, had never written a dramatic scene until he participated in a play-writing workshop which I conducted at his high school in early 1981. I vividly remember Richard's wacky sketch about the trial of someone who had poisoned cans of dog food. I suggested he write something longer, and within a few months he had finished two one-act plays which he submitted to the first Festival. They didn't win, but his next play was *Third Street*. This play was based on something that had actually happened to him: his farewell to some high-school friends after graduation, before leaving for college.

Such an intense memory presents a different kind of challenge to young writers. For example, Jason Brown, the twelve-year-old author of *Tender Places,* said: "The main reason why I wrote this play is because it happened to me . . . it left an imprint on my mind, still dark and powerful today." For some young playwrights, therefore, the first stimulus to writing a play is the need to get something off their chests. People keep a journal for the same reason. But there is a difference between writing something in a private journal and producing it on a stage before hundreds of people. The other three authors in this book—Juan Nunez, Patricia Durkin, and Tagore Joseph McIntyre—had previously written things for publication in school magazines or for literary competitions. They were already used to exposing their ideas in public, so submitting a play to the Young Playwrights Festival was a natural thing for them to do. They did not worry that a huge public would become familiar with their private thinking: in fact, that was the whole point!

Each spring semester every school throughout the country receives a Festival poster which invites young people to "WRITE A PLAY and see it done by top professionals in New York City." The deadline is July 1, by which time our office is deluged with hundreds of scripts, some as short as two pages, some of them hundred-page dramas. From July to November we read all the plays very carefully, writing detailed evaluations of each one. These evaluations are later sent to all writers; they suggest improvements in characterization, dialogue, or dramatic structure, and encourage the writers to continue writing for the theater.

The plays we receive are of every conceivable type and style; they come from authors as young as five or six. Although we do not allow musicals, group-written plays are eligible. We read plays about death or suicide, old age, friendship, sexual relationships, peer or parental problems, sport, historical figures, street life, racism, school, family life, the end of the world, outer space, animals . . . The list is endless. Some of the plays are sophisticated; some imitate the work of other writers; some are TV-style situation comedies or old-fashioned mystery-thrillers; some are very avant-garde (I remember one that just consisted of diagrams); and some are simply truthful versions of everyday life, complete with a fair smattering of street language, dialect, and lively colloquialisms.

The process of selection is quite complicated and takes a long time. A small committee, headed by producing director Peggy C. Hansen, frequently encourages a young writer to submit revisions of a play, with assurances that in doing so, the writer will not jeopardize his or her chances in the contest. This sometimes happens soon after the July deadline. Tagore Joseph McIntyre and I began a lively correspondence, and by November he had sent me, at monthly intervals, three more drafts of *Scraps;* each draft improved on the one before it. Tagore had no play-writing class or workshop to start him off: he did, however, have encouraging parents, and he had his name, inspired by Tagore, the Bengali poet, and Joseph Conrad, the novelist. While some plays are selected without revision, many other plays go through this rewriting process. Peggy's committee makes a preliminary selection of about twenty-five plays out of a total of anywhere from 650 plays, as it did in 1982, to almost 1,200, the number of entries in 1983. In late November Stephen Sondheim chairs an executive selection committee of ten playwrights, all of whom belong to the Dramatists Guild, and these people make the final choice of the eight to ten plays which will be presented in the Festival.

Going to New York

At this point, the winning authors go to New York.

Their wish to see their play done by top professionals has come true; but turning a dream into reality is very hard and very challenging, and it is nothing like school. Many people refer to the Festival as an educational experience, but it is in fact much closer to what the professional theater is about than to any kind of classroom learning. To help the writers understand the obligations of working with professional directors, actors, designers, composers, technicians, and casting and publicity staff, we assign each young playwright a professional writer who acts as an adviser right up to the opening-night performance five months later. The next person the playwright meets is the director who will be responsible for rehearsing the play for an initial reading before an invited audience. This reading, which takes place in December, is a trial run. It is a perfect opportunity to test revisions, and to spend the limited rehearsal time experimenting with the tone of the play.

Sometimes this experiment can become a hairraising introduction to the demands of the professional theater. For example, Peter Getty and his adviser, playwright Wendy Wasserstein, had agreed about certain script changes on the phone, but to Wendy's dismay Peter arrived in the Big Apple with minimal alterations to the play. The director was supposed to begin rehearsals the following day. Where was the final script? Wendy and the director left Peter at his hotel that evening with an ultimatum: a new ending by 7:30 the next morning. During the night Peter rewrote the last third of the play. He scrapped the original title and radically changed his initial concept of the piece.

The great value of the December play readings is that they give the young playwrights a chance to see and hear their plays several months before rehearsals for the actual Festival begin, in April. So there is adequate time to continue working on their scripts. Often this entails clarification and cutting. Writers not only have to be talented; they must also be tenacious, which means remaining patiently unsatisfied until there is a draft that is ready to be tested with skilled professional actors.

The Festival Approaches

In March the young playwrights come to New York a second time. They may have to establish a relationship with a new director; they also continue work on the play with their adviser, attend actors' auditions, and contribute to conferences on set, costume, lighting, and sound designs. Problems inevitably arise: sometimes you have to compromise, and sometimes you have to dig your heels in. The goal is to present, as accurately as possible, the individual vision of each writer. A sudden crisis may require an immediate decision with no time for experimenting. This happened with Jason Brown's *Tender Places*. At the last minute the pivotal role of Sam had to be recast, and there was no time to audition anyone. However, a superb actress cast in one of the other plays was available. The director asked Jason, "What do you think of the idea of Sam as a woman instead of a man?" Jason was startled but said, "Fine. Go ahead, do it."

Charlie Schulman was also asked to be flexible, and to compromise. But he refused to budge. It was very late at night; the dress rehearsal of *The Birthday Present* had been a disaster. The play was almost twenty minutes too long, not very funny, and the forty slides that were projected on the back screen were either in the wrong order or upside down, or too early or too late. Charlie's adviser, A. R. Gurney, Jr., pleaded with Charlie: The play had to be cut. What had the first scene, involving the game of charades, got to do with the rest of the story? Cut it and you saved a good ten minutes. Charlie was adamant: No first scene, no play; the charades stay in. "It's your decision," said Gurney. In the end the slides worked, the pace picked up, and the audiences laughed.

Each writer faces several moments of nail-biting anxiety during the production of his or her play. For Juan Nunez, such a moment was seeing the set for *Meeting the Winter Bike Rider* for the first time.

Everyone seemed delighted with it and showered congratulations on the designer. But Juan was unconvinced by the old-fashioned gas station that had been built for his play: it was too clean. Where was all the dirt, grease, and grime, the dust and the trash? For a long time he sat gloomily, alone in the dark auditorium, wondering why everyone could not see the obvious. He tentatively confided in his director, who reassured him: "It's not finished. It's got to be distressed." "Distressed?" "That means rubbish; muck it up a bit, dust on the windows and shelves, stuff like that."

Patricia Durkin began biting her nails early in rehearsals for *Fixed Up*. Tish heard the actors repeat the lines of her play; at the same time she played back in her mind her own voice saying the same lines. There was a difference: The two sets of voices did not match in rhythm or tone. So Tish turned to her director and repeated the lines, pointing out the nuances and stresses. While the director reassured her, the actors waited patiently: "Please trust us!" they said to themselves. "Give us time to make these lines our own as well as yours!"

During rehearsals for *Third Street* Richard Colman watched the actors abandon his text altogether while his director, Michael Bennett, urged them to improvise. Bennett wanted to shake the actors loose from the text to allow new words to gush forth, new insights. He urged them to discover for themselves the reality of these three young men, high on dope and drink, high on expectations, shared memories, and male comradeship. Richard watched and listened. He wrote new words, no longer exclusively his own but shared among four other people. He wrote, wrote, wrote: long days and nights of improvisation, rewriting and yet more rewriting. His adviser, Michael Weller, urged him to go with the flow, extracting what was good and rejecting the dross. It was a lesson in true collaboration.

Tagore Joseph McIntyre had the interesting experience of seeing adult actors (many of whom were Native American) impersonate the ten-year-old characters in *Scraps* in December and then seeing child actors perform those roles in April.

Joseph Yesutis had a different director and set of actors for the Festival performances. The second production of *Liars* was vastly different in tone. The director whipped the play along at a fast pace so that it was funnier and sharper, bringing out the manipulator in Tom and playing down his self-pity. Consequently the play became less maudlin, and also it was more challenging for audiences. At the discussion following a school matinee most of the high-school students in the audience were deeply moved by Rob and Tom's predicament and shocked by the hypocrisy and cruelty of the boys' peers.

Turning Feelings into Art

The Festival treats the young playwrights as artists who have a great deal of control over their creation. But it is interesting that many of the plays they write depict characters who are miserably isolated, out of control, and painfully aware of it. Three plays in this collection are about friendship, embarrassment, and the possibility of homosexual attraction between young men. Two plays are about school and the hypocrisies and treacheries of that institution. Only one, *Fixed Up,* is a conventional boy-girl play, and it is a comedy riddled with fears and doubts:

> LAURA: You're young, you spend your whole life looking *forward* to something. What if it's nothing?

The three plays about family life (including *The Birthday Present)* are about families at war among themselves.

However, what makes the plays art rather than just a memoir of painful experiences is the authors' ability to distance themselves from their subjects, sometimes with humor, often with a language that is precise, literate, and full of compelling imagery. Here is Mark in MEETING THE WINTER BIKE RIDER:

> Sometimes I feel isolated, so different that I almost think I'm abnormal. I don't think I am, but when I look hard at people, I think that

they're orbiting around me, and when I look
harder, I can see them rip the air.

I think that speech beautifully sums up the feelings
of detachment and dislocation we all have, especially in adolescence. It's a feeling that can be found
in all these plays: it is Benny's misery in *Scraps,*
Alvin's panic in *A New Approach to Human Sacrifice;* as it is Frankie and Ronnie when John's true
feelings have been revealed in *Third Street,* Laura
and Jeffrey in *Fixed Up,* all three boys in *Liars,* and
young Eric in *Tender Places* and his ten-year-old
counterpart Wallace in *The Birthday Present.* Here
is Eric expressing the same feeling of frustration and
abnormality:

Don't be smart, Eric; don't be dumb, Eric.
Don't be sad, Eric. Grow up . . . you're too
young, act your age—you're making me crazy!
MARY: Eric, we want you to see a counselor
. . . psychologist.
ERIC: Oh, no! You make me nuts, then I go
to the shrink?

In fact, it is this kind of angry dislocation and
painful self-awareness that is often the hallmark of a
good writer. It provides a detachment with which to
contemplate unhappiness, and it helps to fashion
this feeling into a play. Writing requires a creative
and vigorous control and a lot of hard work, as we
have seen. But the results are worth it, and that is
why, despite the plays' subject matter, the media
have referred to the Festival as "this most hopeful of

theatrical events" *(New York* magazine), "an evening of glittering optimism for our theater" (Gannett Newspapers). The *New York Times* commented that it "makes one feel hopeful about both the American theater and American young people. . . . Today's theatrical establishment has truly given its sweat and blood to the Young Playwrights Festival. It's a selfless gift whose future dividends are incalculable."

What Happens Now?

Are you inspired to write a play? Inspired by the things you see around you, what has happened to you or to your friends, what you have read, the plays in this book? Whatever it is that inspires you to start, you should know that it is the beginning of an adventure. It might lead to the Festival or beyond.

For some of the playwrights in this book the Festival has led them to continue writing. Peter won a play-writing prize at his college. Joseph, Tish, and Charlie all submitted plays to the Festival the following year. All were rejected; but all continued to write nonetheless, and Charlie turned up again in 1985 with a second winner. Richard wrote two versions of a sequel to *Third Street,* wrote another short play, and then his first full-length work, which his old collaborator, Michael Bennett, wants to direct.

There are regional festivals in California, Ohio, Michigan, Connecticut, Kentucky, Minnesota, and New Jersey. There is even an International Young Playwrights Festival in Australia, which some of the 1985 American winners were invited to attend. The opportunities are there for you. If you are interested in getting more information, or if you want to submit your play (the rule is that you have to be eighteen or under on October 1, the annual deadline), contact:

> The Young Playwrights Festival
> 234 West 44th Street
> New York, New York 10036
> Telephone: (212) 398-9366

Good luck!

THE BIRTHDAY PRESENT
A Play in Three Acts

by Charlie Schulman
(age sixteen when play was written)

CHARACTERS

Wallace Cooper
Mary Cooper
Sheila Cooper
Henry Cooper
Lucy
Alfred Hopp
Newscaster
Joe Finnegan
Talk Show Host
Various Members of Production Crew

ACT ONE
Scene One

The Coopers' living room.

    Today is WALLACE COOPER's *tenth birthday and nobody has shown up for his party yet. The room is decorated for a party. Down right is a small round table with five chairs, each of which has a helium balloon tied to the back. On the table is a paper tablecloth patterned with fire engines or anything else that might be of interest to a group of ten-year-olds. On the table the paper plates, cups, and napkins all match the tablecloth. The party hats can be of any type. Up left and facing the audience diagonally is a very warm, cushy armchair. In front of the armchair is an end table with a drawer and a telephone on it. Behind the armchair is a swinging door leading into the kitchen. Down center is the front door. In between the front door and the party table, facing the armchair, is the couch. As the lights come up,* WALLACE *is sitting on the floor, in the middle of the stage. He is wearing his party hat and sobbing quietly. To his immediate right is a Monopoly set with a game already in progress.*

WALLACE *(still crying):* What time is it, Mom?

MARY *(from the kitchen):* It's almost time, dear.

WALLACE *(crying louder):* How many more minutes?

MARY *(entering):* Actually, Wallace, everybody's five minutes late. But you've got to give them time.

WALLACE: They're not coming! It's gonna be just

like last year. Why do things like this always have to happen to me?

(SHEILA, *Wallace's twelve-year-old sister, enters the room from the kitchen, eating a piece of cake. She flops down on the armchair; her feet dangle over the side.*)

MARY: We can still have the party. There is plenty of food and Daddy will be here soon.
WALLACE: Will Daddy bring me a present?
MARY: Sure, he will.
WALLACE: He will?
MARY: Well, he might.
WALLACE: He won't. *(He starts sobbing again.)*
MARY *(to* SHEILA*)*: I'll go and call him at the office and see if I can catch him there before he leaves. Why don't you try and make Wallace feel a little better? *(She exits into the kitchen.)*
SHEILA: Looks like we are going to have lots of left-over cake. And we can use all the hats and plates from the party you didn't have this year for the party you're not going to have next year. It's your turn to roll the dice.

(WALLACE *picks up the dice from the board.*)

WALLACE: I'm all through not having parties.

(He rolls the dice and moves his piece. SHEILA *slowly slides off the armchair headfirst until she is sitting on the floor.)*

SHEILA: That's Park Place with four houses, that comes to . . .

WALLACE: It doesn't matter. I lose.

SHEILA: You can't quit, I've told you that before. Once you start a game, you have to finish it. Besides, I'm supposed to cheer you up.

WALLACE: But, Sheila, you own all the property, you have all the money; it's not that I want to quit, it's just that I lose.

SHEILA: I'll lend you a thousand bucks. If you have a thousand bucks you're still in the game.

WALLACE: But that's not the way you're supposed to play. I don't have a chance, you're slaughtering me. I quit.

(SHEILA *jumps on top of* WALLACE; *straddling his chest, she grabs him by the collar.*)

SHEILA: You quitter, that's the last time I'm gonna let you play with me.

WALLACE: C'mon, Sheila, let's do something else. Anything you want.

SHEILA *(Her eyes light up):* Anything? *(She loosens her grip.)*

WALLACE: Sure.

SHEILA *(jumping to her feet):* Okay, we're going to play Berlin Wall. I'll go get the mop.

(Pause.)

Loser cleans up.

(She points to the Monopoly game and runs into the kitchen. WALLACE *starts to clean up the game but stops after a few seconds when* SHEILA *reappears with the mop.)*

All right, the couch is the wall, and the chair is freedom.

*(*WALLACE *gets behind the couch.* SHEILA, *who has become the guard, walks back and forth with the mop on her shoulder, singing the "Volga Boatman." When her back is turned,* WALLACE *leaps over the couch and dashes toward the chair.* SHEILA *whirls around and stops him with the mop, pushes him down on the couch, and starts to pummel him.)*

WALLACE: Sheila, stop!
SHEILA: Kill the traitor.
WALLACE: Let's play Monopoly.
SHEILA: Kill, kill, kill.
WALLACE: Mom!

*(*SHEILA *gets off* WALLACE *and sits down next to him.)*

MARY *(from offstage):* What's going on in there?
SHEILA: Nothing, Mom! All you had to say was stop.
WALLACE: I did, I said stop.
SHEILA: You don't have to be a little squealer. I hate squealers.
WALLACE: I'm sorry, Sheila.

SHEILA: Oh, that's okay.

WALLACE: What do you want to play now?

SHEILA: How about boot camp?

WALLACE: No, not boot camp.

SHEILA: How about gestapo?

WALLACE: How does that go?

SHEILA: You sit here

(She points to the armchair)

because you are the prisoner.

WALLACE: What are you?

SHEILA: I'm the gestapo, stupid.

WALLACE: Why do you get to be the gestapo?

SHEILA: Because someone has to do it.

WALLACE: But, but—

SHEILA: Shut up! The game is starting.

(She puts on a German accent.)

What is your name?!

WALLACE: You know my name, Sheila.

SHEILA: C'mon, if you're gonna play, play right.

(She puts on the accent again.)

What is your name?!

WALLACE: Wallace Cooper.

SHEILA: You lie! You lie! *(She slaps him twice, each time on the word "lie.")*

WALLACE: I don't think I want to play this game.

SHEILA: You sure? I kinda like it. . . . All right, I

know what we can do now. You can help me practice my kissing.

WALLACE: Can't we play something else?

SHEILA: I'll tell you what, I'll give you a dollar. But I can't give it to you now, I'll just spend an extra dollar on your birthday present. I haven't gotten it yet.

WALLACE: Nobody has.

SHEILA: All right, so you want to play or not?

WALLACE: Okay.

SHEILA: Sit over here.

(WALLACE *walks back to the couch and sits down next to* SHEILA.)

Okay, here goes.

(*She starts caressing Wallace's face with both hands.*)

WALLACE: What are you doing?

SHEILA: That's what you're supposed to do. It's called foreplay.

WALLACE (*as if a tremendous revelation has hit him*): Ohhh.

(*Suddenly* SHEILA *pulls away and looks in the other direction*)

What are you doing now?

SHEILA: I'm playing hard to get. Girls don't want boys to think that they're cheap.

WALLACE: I don't think you're cheap.

SHEILA: That's exactly what you're supposed to say. You're gonna make a terrific boy someday.

WALLACE: How can you be cheap when you just gave me a dollar?

SHEILA: Okay, Wallace, now you have to pay off.

(She grabs him and gives him the kiss of his life.)

WALLACE: Arrrggghhhh! Arrrggghhhh! You stuck your tongue out!

(He wipes his mouth off with his sleeve.)

Mom! She stuck her tongue out! Disgusting. Disgusting.

(MARY enters.)

MARY: Sheila! Don't stick your tongue out at your brother. You're too old for that kind of silliness. Now, why can't you two play something quiet like charades.

(MARY sits on the couch.)

SHEILA: That's a good idea, let's play charades. But let's have a theme. Ummmmm. How about famous deaths?

(To WALLACE.)

Get out of that chair!

(WALLACE scampers over to the couch. SHEILA kicks off her sneakers and sits on the back of the chair with

her feet on the seat. With a broad grin she starts waving to an imaginary crowd. Suddenly she pretends to get shot and slumps down into the chair.)

MARY: John Kennedy!
WALLACE: Let me go now, let me go now. I've got a good one.

(WALLACE goes over to the table where the party wasn't, and using a knife and fork, he pretends to eat. He starts choking and gagging and finally falls to the floor. Then he sits up.)

Doesn't anyone get it?

(Pause.)

I'm Grandpa Cooper.
MARY: Wallace! If your father heard you say that.
SHEILA: That's disgusting, Wallace, don't you have any class? But that reminds me of a good one.

(SHEILA picks up the mop and, holding it like an ax, starts to pretend to strike her mother with it.)

WALLACE: Lizzie Borden! Everyone knows that.
WALLACE and SHEILA *(singing):*
Lizzie Borden took an ax
and gave her mother forty whacks.
When she saw what she had done,
she gave her father forty-one.
MARY: I think playing this game was a big mistake.

SHEILA: Just one more. I've got a great one.

MARY: All right, one more, but that's it.

(SHEILA, *using a mop, imitates Jesus on the cross and walks around the room in a way that could be mistaken for flying.*)

MARY: Amelia Earhart!

(*After a pause the front door flies open.* DR. HENRY COOPER *stares in wonderment at his crucified daughter.*)

SHEILA (*turning toward her mother*): Dad's home.

(SHEILA *walks back to the armchair.*)
(HENRY *stands in the doorway. In his right hand he carries a rolled-up newspaper. Today he is more depressed than usual.*)

MARY: Henry!

(*She kisses him.*)

Step inside and stay awhile.

(*She laughs at her little joke.* HENRY *steps inside and closes the door.*)

Let me take your coat.

(*She pulls off his right sleeve as* HENRY *passes the newspaper from his right hand to his left. She then pulls off his left sleeve as he passes the newspaper back to his right hand.*)

How was your day, dear?

HENRY *(in a low monotone):* I've decided not to be cremated.

MARY: What?

HENRY: I'll burn when I get there.

MARY: That isn't a very pleasant thing to say.

(HENRY starts to cry. MARY puts his coat on the back of an armchair and guides him to the couch where he sits down.)

What is it? What's the matter?

HENRY *(He opens the newspaper and folds it back):* Read this.

(He hands her the paper)

MARY: What's this all about, Henry?

HENRY: Read it.

MARY *(reading):* "The Personal Practices Committee of the American Medical Association has revoked the license of Dr. Henry Cooper, connecting him with fifteen cases in which Dr. Cooper performed unauthorized experiments on patients at City Hospital. Dr. Cooper—"

HENRY *(interrupting):* Mr. Cooper.

(MARY is startled but regains her composure.)

MARY: "Dr. Cooper claims that his experiments in the area of germ resistance may prove to be a great contribution to the medical world, especially with the growing reality of germ warfare. Cooper's meth-

ods, in which the patient undergoes a series of inoc-
ulations, were rejected by the AMA in the fall of
last year . . ." Is this some kind of joke?

HENRY: No. It's not a joke.

MARY: Then it's a lie, some terrible, filthy lie. You
can never believe what this paper says. Oh, it was
once a good paper until that horrible Australian
bought it.

SHEILA: Sometimes they tell the truth.

HENRY: I was so close.

(He starts crying again.)

So close. It only takes eight weeks to finish. Then I
could have proved to them that they were wrong
about me.

MARY: It says here that you said even if you com-
pleted the procedure it might take years before we
could find out if it really worked.

HENRY: Don't you understand that I'm sitting on
something really big?

(He thinks about that for a few seconds.)

I'm the only one that believes in it, the only one.
Some people only get one really good idea in their
whole lives and this is mine. Can you understand
that?

SHEILA: Dad, did you get Wallace a present? It's his
birthday, you know.

WALLACE: He didn't, he forgot; everyone forgot.

(He starts crying again.)

SHEILA: Did you forget to buy Wallace a present?
HENRY: A present?

(He starts to space out.)

MARY: Sheila, can't you see that your father is very upset about something?
HENRY: Of course I did. Of course I got Wallace a present.
WALLACE: You did?
HENRY: Yes, I did.
WALLACE: Can I have it?
HENRY: Sure . . . but not today.
WALLACE: Not today?
HENRY: Tomorrow. Tomorrow morning.
WALLACE: Are you sure you have it?
HENRY: Yes, I have it. Now, be patient and I'll give it to you in the morning.
MARY *(becoming very upset):* Why couldn't you tell me about all this before? Why did you have to wait until it came out in the papers? I don't understand how you could throw away your whole career like that. I don't understand what those experiments were all about, but doing them after you were not supposed to is wrong. Can't you understand that it's wrong?
SHEILA: But Daddy is always right and Mommy is always wrong. Didn't you know that?
MARY: Be quiet, Sheila.

SHEILA: Daddy was right when he married Mommy, but Mommy was wrong when she married Daddy.

HENRY: That's enough out of you, Sheila. Now finish that article, Mary.

MARY: There's more?

HENRY: That's right, there's more.

MARY *(looking back at the newspaper):* It says—it says, "Dr. Cooper is also facing criminal charges."

(They all look around at one another.)

SHEILA *(skipping around the room and singing):* Daddy is going to jail, Daddy is going to jail.

HENRY: Shut up, Sheila!!!

BLACKOUT

Scene Two

The Coopers' living room.

It is the next morning. HENRY *is sitting in the armchair talking on the telephone to his lawyer. He is in a bathrobe and slippers.*

HENRY: The twenty-third? It is just not long enough. I need more time. But, Burt, I'm not asking you to win this case for me. I just want you to get me another postponement. I need the time.

(WALLACE *enters in his pajamas.*)

WALLACE: Dad?

(HENRY *gives* WALLACE *the "be quiet" sign and puts his hand on the boy's shoulder.*)

HENRY: July seventeenth? . . . Perfect.

(*He circles the wall calendar just above the telephone.*)

That's in exactly eight weeks. . . . You don't think there'll be any problem, do you? . . . Great. . . . Forget this case, Burt, it's a lost cause. I just needed the postponement. Okay, thanks a lot. Sorry for calling so early in the morning. Good-bye.

(*He hangs up the phone.*)

Hi, Wallace. I was thinking about you a lot last night.

WALLACE: You were?

HENRY: Yes, I was. I guess you're pretty upset about your party yesterday, so I made this sign for you.

(*He opens the top drawer of the end table and takes out a small cardboard sign with a piece of string attached at both ends.*)

You can wear it to school. It says, "My name is Wallace Cooper and I would like for someone in this class to be my friend. Thank you."

(He hangs it around Wallace's neck.)

WALLACE: Thanks, Dad. . . . This isn't my present, is it?

HENRY *(laughing):* No, it isn't.

WALLACE: Do you have my present?

HENRY *(smiling):* Yes, I do, son.

WALLACE: Can I have it?

HENRY *(seriously):* You have to promise me one thing first. You won't tell anybody about this present—not Mommy, not Sheila, not anybody. That's why I waited until we could be alone before I gave it to you.

WALLACE: I promise.

HENRY: Now, Wallace, the present I'm about to give you isn't a toy.

WALLACE: It isn't?

HENRY: No. As a matter of fact it's going to take two months to give it to you.

WALLACE: Two months?

HENRY: I know this is hard for you to understand, but this present hurts.

WALLACE: It hurts?

HENRY: Then it helps.

WALLACE: It hurts?

HENRY: Yes, but when you grow up you'll thank me, I promise.

(HENRY takes out a syringe from the drawer, fills it up with a liquid, and spurts a little out through the needle.)

WALLACE: Is that my present?
HENRY: Yes.
WALLACE: I think I'm late for school.

(WALLACE *backs away.*)

HENRY: Wallace, I'm not going to chase after you.
. . . Come here, Son, it will only take a second.
WALLACE: I don't want to.
HENRY: If you don't do this for me, if you don't come over here, you'll be no son of mine.

(WALLACE *walks over to his father and puts his hand on the arm of the chair.*)

You're going to have to trust me, Wallace. It might take ten, fifteen, even twenty years, but one day you'll thank me.

(HENRY *rolls up the boy's sleeve. The lights fade to black as he injects him.*)

ACT TWO
Scene One

Wallace's apartment.

Twenty years have passed. Today is Wallace's thirtieth birthday. The stage is now in two parts. On the left side is Wallace's apartment. All the furniture has been taken out of the apartment by Wallace's wife, LUCY, *and her lawyer,* ALFRED HOPP. *Strewn about the room are boxes filled with books, records, etc. All that is left in the room is a small television set on the floor; it faces* HOPP. *Down left, up against the side wall, is a window with a small cactus on the sill. On the other side of the TV sits the* NEWSCASTER *in the dark. Behind him is a screen for slides to be projected on. As the lights come up on Wallace's apartment, both* LUCY *and* HOPP *are sitting on boxes.* HOPP *has his briefcase open on his lap.*

HOPP *(taking out a sandwich wrapped in tinfoil):* I hope you don't mind if I eat my lunch while we're waiting for your husband?

LUCY: Not at all. Do what you like.

HOPP: Thank you.

(He takes a light beer and a can opener out of his briefcase. With some difficulty he opens the beer, puts the can opener back in the briefcase, and takes out a piece of chocolate cake wrapped in cellophane. Balancing the sandwich on one knee, the cake on the other, and the beer between his legs, he takes out a paper napkin that has been folded sixteen times, and carefully unfolds it. Using his briefcase as a table, he

meticulously smooths the napkin and then strategically places his food on it.)

Lately I've been eating on the run most of the time. No time for peace and quiet. Always another miserable marriage to attend to. People paying me to help them get away from each other. It just doesn't seem right.

(He looks deeply into his roast beef sandwich.)

I like my roast beef rare. If you cook it too much it stops bleeding.

(He tears into his sandwich viciously.)

I could never be a vegetarian, couldn't imagine spending my whole life just eating plants. As for me, if I don't eat meat for a couple of days, I get irritable. I gotta sink my teeth into something bloody every once in a while or I just don't act myself.

LUCY: I guess that makes for a good divorce lawyer.

HOPP: I guess so.

(He laughs uproariously.)

LUCY: I wonder where Wallace is? I hope he hasn't forgotten.

HOPP *(unwrapping his cake):* That would be pretty funny.

(WALLACE *enters.)*

He'd walk in here and we'd say "Surprise!"

WALLACE: I—I don't know what to say. I am surprised. A party, beer, cake, guest. I never expected this in a million years. Thanks, Lucy; thanks, Lucy. Thanks for remembering my birthday.

LUCY: Today is your birthday?

WALLACE: I've never had a birthday party before.

LUCY: I'm sorry, Wallace, I've made a terrible mistake. Didn't I tell you that I was coming over with my lawyer to have you sign the divorce papers?

WALLACE: No, you didn't.

LUCY: I feel so foolish.

WALLACE: It's okay.

LUCY: I'm such an idiot.

WALLACE: No, it's okay, really, I'm used to it. What happened to the furniture?

LUCY: It's gone. I've taken back everything that was mine. And, well, everything was mine, except for the TV. This is my lawyer.

HOPP (interrupting): Alfred Hopp at your service

(He shakes hands with WALLACE.)

or should I say at your wife's service. Have you gotten yourself a lawyer, Mr. Cooper?

WALLACE: No, I haven't. But I guess I should.

HOPP: Well, here's my card just in case you ever get divorced again.

WALLACE: Divorced again?

LUCY: We brought the papers. I signed them; now we need you to.

HOPP: I have them right here.

(He stands up, puts his food down on a box, and takes the papers from his briefcase. With a pen that he has removed from his breast pocket, he presents them to WALLACE *who doesn't respond in any way.)*

LUCY *(whispering):* Wallace?

*(*HOPP *and* LUCY *look at him, then at each other.)*

WALLACE: You took all the furniture?

LUCY: Except the TV.

*(*WALLACE *turns on the TV, sits down on a box, and starts to watch.* LUCY *and* HOPP *look at the TV and around the room; they don't know what to do.)*

WALLACE: The TV?

LUCY: You can't do this, Wallace.

WALLACE: I wasn't expecting to get divorced today. I'm really not up for it.

LUCY: Wait a second, when I asked you to marry me last year, I told you we'd get divorced in a year, and you agreed.

WALLACE: I know, but . . .

LUCY: I offered you four thousand dollars, that was the going rate; but you said you'd marry me as a favor and wouldn't accept any money. I should have made you take it.

WALLACE: I couldn't take any money from you.

LUCY: That's very nice of you, Wallace, but just because you like me doesn't mean I owe you anything. I don't want to hurt your feelings, but you wouldn't want to force me to be married to you, would you? I wanna go out and be on my own. I'm a citizen now. I have my green card.

(Looking at the audience.)

Yugoslavia seems so far away. Please sign these papers, Wallace, please?

WALLACE: I don't think I should.

LUCY: What do you mean, you don't think you should? This is pathetic, this is really pathetic.

WALLACE: Could you step out of the way? You're blocking the TV.

HOPP: May I have a word with you alone, Mrs. Cooper?

(They walk to the other side of the room.)

Of course, you do realize that your husband deciding not to sign the divorce papers is an unexpected development, and since it will take quite a bit of coercion on my part to change his mind, I must inform you that my fee is no longer fixed.

LUCY: You told me last year that I would have no problem.

HOPP: I believe that I said you *should* have no problem. But really, Mrs. Cooper, surely you must know that not even a lawyer can predict the future. Now, if you would just leave me alone with your husband for a few minutes, I'm sure I could convince him to change his mind.

LUCY: If you think I should.

HOPP: Believe me, I've dealt with these kind of guys before.

(He picks up her coat and hands it to her. LUCY puts it on and he guides her to the door, which he opens.)

Now say good-bye to your husband.

(She doesn't say anything.)

Say good-bye!

LUCY: Good-bye, Wallace.

(WALLACE waves good-bye without looking away from the TV screen.)

HOPP: I'll let you know how everything works out.

(He closes the door.)

Well, Mr. Cooper, it seems we have a little problem here. Your wife has made it clear that she wants a divorce.

WALLACE: It's just a misunderstanding.

HOPP: This is not a misunderstanding, believe me; I've been divorced before.

WALLACE: Maybe she'll change her mind.

HOPP: Listen to me, son. You're young, single, and mildly attractive. You're too young to be tied down for the rest of your life. You should follow my example, Wallace. Divorce has been the best thing that ever happened to me in my life. Look, you seem like a nice young man. I'm sorry to do this to you. You don't think I do this job because I like it, do you? It makes me feel guilty whenever I go to a wedding. As a present, I refer them to a good marriage counselor; it's the least I can do. The truth is that I do my job for the money. I'm not ashamed to say it; I need the money.

NEWSCASTER: *(The lights come up.)* We interrupt this program so that we can bring you a special report.

WALLACE: Hey, a special report. I love those.

NEWSCASTER: We have just received word from reliable sources in Morocco that no births have been reported in that country for the past two days.

HOPP: Turn up the volume.

(As WALLACE *turns up the sound, the* NEWSCASTER *begins to speak louder.)*

NEWSCASTER: Other countries in North Africa have reported a major decrease in pregnancies and births. A search of the region for pregnant women is getting under way. Specialists are now being flown in to Rabat, Morocco's capital city, in the hope of combating this dreadful epidemic which may be threatening the existence of mankind. We repeat, a major wave of infertility has been reported to be sweeping most of North Africa. We will keep you informed of the latest developments coming out of the area.

(WALLACE *pressed the off button and the lights fade on the* NEWSCASTER.)

WALLACE *(after a pause):* So that's why Ingrid Bergman left Humphrey Bogart in *Casablanca.*

HOPP: Now I get it! How could I have been so stupid? I know what you're doing, you're holding out for a cash settlement, right?

WALLACE: Well, uh, I—actually, no.

HOPP: C'mon, don't kid me. I know you're out of a job, and I also know that there's no great demand for pipe fitters either.

WALLACE: I don't need your money.

HOPP: Don't give me that! Everybody needs money! You look like you could use some new furniture around here. How about if I fix you up with my sister. If you ever decide to get married, I'll do the divorce for free.

WALLACE: But I really like Lucy. She can be a lot of fun when she's not divorcing you. Haven't you ever heard of love?

HOPP: Love!? Well, if you're going to be like that, Mr. Cooper, I'm afraid that I will have to settle this in court.

BLACKOUT

Scene Two

Lights come up on the NEWSCASTER.

NEWSCASTER: Ladies and gentlemen, one week after first reporting to you of the wave of infertility in North Africa, we regret to inform you that no pregnancies have been reported on the continent of Africa today. Scientists are still baffled by the cause of this epidemic. What they do know is that whatever this disease is, it is very contagious. They have also determined—

(Looks up.)

and this is a major point—that infertility is occurring in males only. To make matters worse, births and pregnancies are down in the United States as well as in many other countries. On a good note, this disease has had no effect on livestock or wildlife. The reason for this—well, your guess is as good as mine. The big question in the world today is, What or who is the cause of this problem? Fingers are being pointed at the United States and the Soviet Union.

(A slide of the United States is projected on the screen behind the NEWSCASTER; *the word* oops! *is written across it.)*

It is believed that both of these countries have been experimenting with germ warfare, and perhaps one of them has made a mistake which has triggered this worldwide catastrophe. The State Department has issued a statement claiming that they have not experimented with germ warfare since the forties and that this is probably some misguided Soviet plot aimed at the destruction of the free world. The Kremlin said today that they, too, have not experimented in this area since the forties, and claimed that this is an imperialist plot from the West which, at the beginning, was aimed at the destruction of the Third World but somehow got out of hand. Said one official from the State Department who wished to remain unidentified, "We believe that aliens from another planet may be responsible, and we will look seriously into this possibility." The president has asked that all male American citizens and noncitizens, "who should not fear deportation," comply with a nationwide semen evaluation by bringing a personal sample to their local hospital.

BLACKOUT

Scene Three

Wallace's apartment, one week later.

WALLACE *is sitting on a box, reading a copy of* Field and Stream. LUCY *opens the door with her key and enters.*

WALLACE: Lucy, what brings you here?

LUCY: I've come to take back my boxes.

WALLACE: Have a seat; would you like something to drink?

LUCY: No, thanks, I'm in kind of a hurry.

(She starts collecting the boxes.)

WALLACE: Want me to help you with those boxes?

LUCY: No, that's okay.

(JOE FINNEGAN enters.)

Joe is gonna help me.

WALLACE: Joe?

LUCY: Joe, this is my husband, Wallace Cooper. Wallace, this is Joe Finnegan.

WALLACE: Hi.

(The two men shake hands; JOE's grip hurts WALLACE.)

LUCY: Joe used to work for the Secret Service.

JOE: Shhh!

LUCY: Sorry, I forgot.

JOE: I used to protect the president, but they fired me when he got shot.

LUCY: They said it was his fault. It wasn't, Joe; it wasn't your fault.

JOE: I was way out of position, never even got a chance to throw myself in front of a bullet, so now I'm out of a job, and to make matters worse, I have to worry about being sterile. Ya know, Wallace, all my life women have fallen all over me like I was going out of style. But just yesterday I was rapping with this chick and she wasn't interested. That's never happened to me before. It was like she could tell that I was sterile. I don't know, maybe I'm losing my confidence. Maybe I'm losing my scent. Can you see what I'm trying to get at?

LUCY: Joe?

(JOE *looks at* LUCY *as if he just noticed that she was in the room.)*

LUCY: I think we should be bringing those boxes downstairs.

JOE: I got 'em.

WALLACE: So I see that you're running around with unemployed bodyguards.

LUCY: It's a free country, isn't it?

WALLACE: You may have forgotten, but we are still married.

LUCY: Just call my lawyer and we can change all that.

(LUCY *exits. The lights dim. A slide appears behind the* NEWSCASTER. *It shows a naked man with his arms extended and his groin area blacked out. The word "Infertility" is written in large letters at the bottom of the slide.*)

NEWSCASTER: The feeling is one of helplessness and despair in America and all over the world today. No pregnancies have been reported anywhere. All birth control manufacturers and distributors have folded, leaving thousands jobless. Abortion is no longer an issue. For a short time it was believed that sperm banks held the answer to this predicament. However, scientists have confirmed that there is no defense against contamination from bacteria causing sterilization.

(*Lights come up on Wallace's apartment where* WALLACE *is sitting on the floor watching TV. Then lights come up on* HENRY COOPER *Stage Right. He is lying on a fold-up beach chair. He is bare-chested and is drinking a Bloody Mary with a celery stalk in it.* HENRY *picks up the telephone and starts to dial. The phone rings in Wallace's apartment.*)

WALLACE: Hello?
HENRY: Hello, Wallace?
WALLACE: Yeah?
HENRY: This is it.

WALLACE: What do you mean this is it? Who is this?

HENRY: I've waited a long time for this day to come. Now your birthday present starts to pay off.

WALLACE: Dad?

HENRY: That's right, it's me.

WALLACE: Dad, where have you been? We haven't seen or heard from you in ten years, not since you broke out of prison. Where are you?

HENRY: Somewhere in South America. I can't tell you where. I'm still wanted, you know. How's your mother?

WALLACE: She divorced you, Dad.

HENRY: Yeah, I figured she would.

WALLACE: She married a dentist and moved to Arizona.

HENRY: A dentist! I thought the woman had more class than that. I guess you never really know a person. What about your sister?

WALLACE: Sheila? She went to Africa seven years ago. She's teaching the finer points of guerrilla warfare to the Tanzanian army.

HENRY: Sounds like something Sheila would do. Have you been paying attention to the news lately?

WALLACE: Who hasn't . . . it's pretty strange.

HENRY: Did you do what the president told you to —I mean, go down to the hospital?

WALLACE: Sure I did. Everybody has.

HENRY: Did you get your results back?

WALLACE: No, not yet, but I figure I—

HENRY *(interrupting):* Good! Good! I'm glad I got to you first. Now listen to me, Wallace, this may be hard for you to believe, but . . .

(Long pause.)

you are the last fertile man in the whole world.

WALLACE *(looking down at his crotch):* Are you kidding me?

HENRY *(very distinctly):* I am not kidding. *(He starts to laugh.)*

WALLACE: You mean those shots you gave me before you went to jail?

HENRY: Yes, happy birthday, Son.

WALLACE: D-dad, you didn't do the procedure with anyone else, did you?

HENRY: What?! No! I wouldn't do something like that and spoil all your fun. Of course I tried to before they put me in jail. So you're the only one. You know, I have the cure for this little problem the world is having.

WALLACE: That's great, Dad, you'll be a big hero. You'll go down in history as the greatest man in history.

HENRY: I know, I know, but why so fast? What's the big hurry? Look, they'll make the connection between you and me immediately, but what good will it do them? Nobody knows where I am. I could be dead.

WALLACE: What are you trying to say?

HENRY: Say I resurface. I show everyone the cure,

and the world returns to normal, no big deal. *(Pause.)* But let's say that I stay right here in South America. Imagine it: You're the only man in the world that can impregnate women. The whole god-damn world. Think of the power you'll have. It'll be up to you to keep the human race going. And this is the part I like most of all. You get to start the world over, Wallace, and in eighty years every single person will be one of our descendants. Talk about a family operation.

WALLACE: Do you think people will be better off?

HENRY: I don't know if they'll be better off, but at least they'll be better looking. *(He laughs very loudly.)*

WALLACE: Dad?

HENRY: Yes?

WALLACE: How can we be sure that my son will be fertile?

HENRY: I'm glad you asked that question. Hopefully, you'll be able to genetically pass on your immunities to your sons. It worked with drosophila, mice, and even chimpanzees, so if it worked with them, it should work with you. Of course, there is a possibility that it won't work. But that's what makes life interesting, right?

WALLACE: I guess so.

HENRY: Well, good-bye, kid. I expect the CIA will be out looking for me soon, so I've got to keep one step in front of them. *(He sips his Bloody Mary.)*

Good luck, Wallace, and watch out for those European women.

WALLACE: I haven't been having very much luck with them lately.

HENRY: I'm sure you haven't been having very much luck with any women lately. But all that's going to change now, because of what I've done for you.

WALLACE: I hope so.

HENRY: Good-bye, I've really got to go. *(He hangs up.)*

WALLACE: Good-bye. *(He hangs up. A big smile comes across Wallace Cooper's face.)*

(Lights come up on NEWSCASTER.)

NEWSCASTER: Word has just reached the newsroom that a fertile man has been found in New York City.

(A slide of WALLACE appears.)

His name is Wallace Cooper. Now, you all must be wondering why Mr. Cooper has not fallen victim to this strange epidemic which has already had a devastating impact upon the people of this planet. It seems that Mr. Cooper's fertility may be connected with experiments performed by his father over twenty years ago. A worldwide dragnet is now getting under way in the hope of finding Dr. Cooper, who is still at large. So, Dr. Cooper, if you're out there listening, please, sir, make yourself known, the world needs you. Until then, Wallace Cooper, the fate of the human race is in your hands.

(Focus shifts to Wallace's apartment. SHEILA *enters. She is dressed in an African robe and is holding two large suitcases.)*

SHIELA: Hi, Wallace, it's me, Sheila, your sister. Remember me?

WALLACE: Well sure, yeah, of course I remember.

SHELIA: That's not a very enthusiastic welcome. Aren't you glad to see me?

WALLACE: Sure I am, but I'm kind of, well, ah, I'm . . .

SHELIA: Speak up, Wallace. *(She puts down her suitcases.)*

WALLACE: I said I've been kinda overwhelmed by everything that has happened today.

SHELIA: Took the first flight out of Dar es Salaam as soon as I heard.

WALLACE: I just talked to Dad on the phone.

SHELIA: Oh, yeah, how is he?

WALLACE: Fine.

SHEILA: Is he still in jail?

(She opens her suitcase and starts replacing the paintings on the wall with African wall hangings.)

WALLACE: No, Sheila, he escaped ten years ago.

SHELIA: Oh, yeah, I forgot. What about Mom?

WALLACE: She married a dentist and moved to Arizona.

SHELIA: Oh . . . *(Pause.)* You know I always thought that Dad was a really sick guy who didn't know what he was doing, but I guess I was wrong. Either that or he was very lucky.

WALLACE: So what are you doing while you're in town?

SHELIA: I've decided to become your agent. You need one, don't you?

WALLACE: Well, I . . .

SHELIA: Don't mention it, that's what sisters are for. Now, what I need to know is what exactly is our policy going to be about artificial insemination?

WALLACE: I don't think we should. I mean, that way it could fall into the wrong hands, and we don't want that. Personal delivery seems to be the best way.

SHEILA: I agree. I've already scheduled you for two appointments tomorrow. Mrs. Hilton was sitting next to me on the plane, and we have her scheduled for nine A.M.

(WALLACE *starts doing push-ups.*)

I took the liberty of charging her a million dollars without asking you first. Is that okay? What are you doing?

WALLACE: Getting in shape.

SHEILA: Are you listening?

WALLACE: Yeah, Hilton at nine, and a million is fine.

SHEILA: At ten-thirty we have the wife of the oil

minister of Kuwait. We're charging her two million; her husband can afford it. Of course, later you're gonna have to do some freebies so we don't get poor people angry at us. After all, we can't just have a society of rich people. I mean, what's the point of being rich when there is no one around to be poor. And I almost forgot, we are having a press conference at twelve.

(The phone rings and SHEILA *answers it.)*

Hello. . . . Wallace, it's the president. Would you hold on a minute, please.

(She hands him the phone. WALLACE *speaks into the phone.)*

WALLACE: No, Mr. President, I haven't decided whether I'd sleep with communists. . . . No, I don't think that it would mean I was a traitor if I did. In fact, I think it would improve relations. . . . No, sir, I haven't decided about the Third World either. Isn't this a free country? . . . Oh, I see. Your wife? Isn't she kind of old? How about your daughter?

(The doorbell rings.)

Okay, speak to my agent.

*(*WALLACE *hands the phone to* SHEILA *and goes to open the door.* JOE FINNEGAN *stands there in his*

three-piece suit; he is wearing sunglasses and carries a walkie-talkie.)

What are you doing here?

JOE: The president has assigned me to protect you.

SHEILA *(speaking into the phone):* We can fit your daughter in at eleven. *(She hangs up the phone.)*

WALLACE: What do I need to be protected from?

JOE: Have you looked outside?

(WALLACE goes to look out.)

Stay away from that window.

(JOE jumps in between WALLACE and the window. Phone rings and SHEILA answers it.)

You can look over my shoulder.

(WALLACE, on tiptoe, peeks over Joe's shoulder.)

WALLACE: Wow! There's thousands of women out there.

(SHEILA hangs up the phone.)

Who was that?

SHEILA: *Time* magazine. They want you for next week's cover, a picture of you next to a picture of George Washington, with a caption reading "The future father of our country."

WALLACE: Future father of our country. I like that, it has a nice ring to it. I cannot tell a lie; it was I who got your wife pregnant.

SHEILA *(noticing* JOE): Who's that?

WALLACE: Oh, Sheila, this is Joe Finnegan, my bodyguard and my wife's lover. Joe, this is my older sister and agent, Sheila Cooper.

(They shake hands, but SHEILA *doesn't let go.)*

SHEILA *(to* WALLACE): Your wife? What's all this about a wife?

WALLACE: Lucy? She's from Yugoslavia. She married me so that she could get her green card. Now she wants a divorce, but I wouldn't sign the papers.

SHEILA: You wouldn't sign the papers?

(She starts shaking him back and forth.)

Of all the stupid. I should have realized that you're still an imbecile. Some things never change. *(She lets go.)*

(ALFRED HOPP enters and JOE frisks him.)

Who's that?

WALLACE: That's Lucy's lawyer, Alfred Hopp.

(LUCY enters and waves a brown paper bag in Joe's face.)

LUCY: I brought you some lunch.

JOE *(to* LUCY): Could you raise your arms in the air, I'm going to have to frisk you.

SHEILA *(smiling):* Hello, Mr. Hopp. I'm Sheila Cooper, Wallace's agent.

HOPP: Nice to meet you.

(They shake hands.)

JOE: Mr. Cooper, can I have my lunch break?
WALLACE: Sure.
SHEILA: Well, Mr. Hopp, I've talked to Wallace and I've been able to convince him to sign those divorce papers.
HOPP: I'm afraid that will be impossible.

(JOE *is still frisking* LUCY.)

LUCY: Not here, Joe.
HOPP: My client has informed me that she is no longer solely interested in obtaining a divorce.

(JOE *starts kissing Lucy's neck; he makes animal noises.*)

WALLACE: What does that mean?
SHEILA: It means she wants your money.
WALLACE: But I just got it. I mean I was just about to get it. That's not very nice.
HOPP: Adultery isn't very nice either, Mr. Cooper.
WALLACE: Adultery? I haven't done anything yet. She wanted the divorce in the first place. Besides, what about her? She's the one committing adultery.

(Joe's animal noises become louder.)

HOPP: That will be very hard to pin on them. Mr. Finnegan is undercover and you are an international figure. Everyone knows about you and Mrs. Hilton, it's all over the news. Frankly, I think what you're planning to do is disgusting and immoral. It's unfortunate that it had to come to this, but you leave me no choice. I'm afraid the next time we meet will have to be in court.

SHEILA: You really got us into a mess this time.

BLACKOUT

ACT THREE

A TV studio.

It is ten months later. The stage is set up for a talk show. Four black swivel chairs are lined up next to one another. The talk show HOST *sits on the chair on the far left. About ten feet to the left of the* HOST *a curtain hangs from the ceiling creating an offstage onstage. Standing by the talk show* HOST *are* JOE FINNEGAN *in full bodyguard attire,* SHEILA, *and* WALLACE.

HOST: Ladies and gentlemen, today history will be made on this show. As some of you may know, last night authorities found Dr. Henry Cooper in Peru. The doctor, who is being heavily guarded backstage, has consented to come out on stage and tell us a few things, like where he has been all this time and how come he didn't turn himself in. Immediately following this show Dr. Cooper will be whisked away to City Hospital where he will explain to a jam-packed lecture room of specialists the cure to this wave of sterility which struck the world a little over ten months ago. Also joining us this evening are two other members of the Cooper family. May I introduce to you a woman who has unselfishly stayed behind the scene because, well, she's just that kind of person, and boy, do we need some of them. Wallace's sister and press agent, Sheila Cooper.

(SHEILA *walks in. The* HOST *gets up and steps one chair to the right. They shake hands.* SHEILA *kisses him on the cheek. They laugh and smile. She kisses him again; they sit down.)*

Tell me, Sheila, what was your first reaction to finding out that your brother was the last fertile man?

SHEILA: Well, I was in Africa when Wallace called me. He told me that he needed me to help him. We've always been a close family, so of course I dropped everything and flew here to be with him.

HOST: I must ask you this question, Sheila.

SHEILA *(smiling):* Please do.

HOST: How did the divorce case affect you and Wallace?

SHEILA: Let's just say that it was unfortunate that the divorce had to be so nasty and bitter. Of course, it was emotionally draining, not to mention all the money we lost. But I would like to say—and I'm sure I speak for Wallace—that we think Lucy is a fine young lady and we wish her all the best. I just hope for her sake that she never runs into me in the street because I'll—

HOST *(interrupting):* Um, ah, let's bring Wallace in now.

SHEILA: Certainly.

HOST: And now a man who needs no introduction, a man who as a ten-year-old had no friends but has plenty now . . . let me introduce Wallace Cooper.

(WALLACE enters; the HOST stands and moves one seat over. WALLACE shakes his hand but does not acknowledge his sister. They both sit down.)

Tell me, Wallace, how do you feel about having thirty-six girls and no boys?

WALLACE: Well, of course, it's depressing. It puts a lot of pressure on me, but that has eased up now that my father has shown up to save the world. . . . But yes, people are getting angry about that.

HOST: How do you explain it?

WALLACE: How do I explain it? Well, I can't really. I'm pretty sure that it's just a coincidence. I'm still expecting to have a son any day now.

HOST: And on that note let's break for a commercial and come back with Wallace Cooper's father.

(HOST *looks up to the lighting crew.*)

MEMBER OF THE LIGHTING CREW: We're off the air. Two minutes, everybody.

(ALFRED HOPP *runs on stage.*)

HOPP: Wallace.

(WALLACE *walks over to him.*)

Miss America just had a baby.

WALLACE: Yeah, so what is it?

HOPP: It's a . . . girl.

WALLACE: A girl?

HOPP: Sorry.

WALLACE: Thirty-seven? I can't believe it.

HOPP: Miss America is a client of mine, and we are suing you for breach of contract.

WALLACE: What!! I got her pregnant, didn't I?

HOPP: That's true, you did. But the reason you impregnated these women was to keep the race going. But that can't happen if there aren't any boys.

WALLACE: I don't guarantee boys.

HOPP: I know, but you've had thirty-seven daughters; obviously there's something wrong with you and you can't spawn males.

WALLACE: But if you sue me and win, then everyone will sue me. I'll be right back where I started.

HOPP: Sorry, Wallace, this time you lose.

(He exits through the back way.)

MEMBER OF THE LIGHTING CREW: One minute!

(HENRY COOPER *runs onstage.)*

HENRY: Wallace, I've got to talk to you. *(He takes him aside.)* I have something to confess.

WALLACE: Well?

HENRY: I—I don't know the cure.

WALLACE: What!

HENRY: Shhhhh!

WALLACE: What are you talking about?

HENRY: I don't know the cure. I just know the prevention. There's a big difference.

WALLACE: Why did you wait till now to tell me?

HENRY: I wanted to be a big hero. I didn't want to let the world down.

WALLACE: God damn it, Dad, we are on international television.

MEMBER OF THE LIGHTING CREW: Ten seconds.

HENRY: Don't worry, I'll talk my way out of it.

WALLACE: You've got to be kidding. This is crazy!

(WALLACE *walks back to his seat and sits down with his head in his hands.* SHEILA *makes him sit up straight.*)

MEMBER OF THE LIGHTING CREW: Five, four, three, two, one. You're on.

HOST: And now the moment you've all been waiting for. The most respected man in the world. May I introduce Dr. Henry Cooper.

(SHEILA, HOST, FINNEGAN, *all give* COOPER *a standing ovation.* WALLACE *stands up late and claps along.* HENRY *waves to crowd, shakes host's hand and sits down.*)

It's a pleasure to meet you, Dr. Cooper.

HENRY: Not at all.

HOST: No really, the world is happy to see you.

HENRY: Is that so? They didn't seem very happy twenty-five years ago when they took away my license and sent me to jail. That wasn't a very happy experience.

HOST: That may be true but—

HENRY: But nothing. That's what's wrong with people today, they don't take you for what you are. Only after you do something great do they treat you with any respect. I'm the same person as I was before. Only now I'll be accepted in the scientific world. I hate those people who, when you're young and unknown, won't listen to a word you say, treat you like a nobody. But they're the same guys who kiss your ass when you finally make it. I've got it all up here. *(He points to his head.)* It's not written down anywhere, and now after everything it's done to me, the world is now dying for my knowledge. Well, let me tell you something, I don't owe the world anything and I don't feel like telling them a damn thing.

HOST: But you can't do that, sir, we're talking about the survival of mankind. The world won't let you get away with it. We'll beat it out of you.

(HOST *starts to roll up his sleeves.)*

DR. COOPER: I've already thought about that, but the world does not deserve to live. They'll probably blow themselves up anyway. Having the race just get old and die seems the best way . . . that's why I've decided to take this cyanide pill.

(He holds up the pill. They all lunge for him, but he eats it and dies immediately.)

SHEILA: Oh, my God.

WALLACE *(taking his pulse):* He's dead. *(Looking at his father.)* I can't believe you did this.

HOST: That's it, ladies and gentlemen, the future of mankind has just ended and you saw it right here on *The Bill Johnson Hour.* Well, everybody, this is your host, Bill Johnson, saying good-bye for myself

(He looks at HENRY COOPER.*)*

and my guests. See you

(He points to the audience.)

next week.

(He holds this pose.)

Are we off?

CREW MEMBER: Yep.

HOST *(jumping out of his seat):* Jesus Christ! Jesus Christ! Goddamn son of a bitch!! I wonder if this will have any bearing on my career. On the other hand, maybe this could help. I mean all the exposure. But this isn't what I want to be known for! I don't want to become a trivia question!

WALLACE: I think we should move the body.

HOST *(whirling toward* WALLACE): You shut up! This is very confusing. *(To* JOE.) Hey, you! Come over here and make yourself useful! Help me get this stiff out of my studio! Of all the rotten luck.

*(*JOE *takes the arms and the* HOST *takes the legs, and they start to carry Henry's body off.* ALFRED HOPP *runs onstage.)*

HOPP: Wallace, that wife of the Brazilian coffee plantation owner just had a baby!

WALLACE: And?

HOPP: It's a bouncing baby boy!

WALLACE: It's a boy!

(WALLACE *walks over to his father's body and, standing between the* HOST *and* JOE *who are carrying* HENRY, *reaches into his pocket and pulls out a cigar.)*

Have a cigar, Dad!

(He puts the cigar between Henry's lips.)

BLACKOUT

CHARLIE SCHULMAN

I'm a native New Yorker presently attending the University of Michigan where I have been the recipient of the Avery Hopwood Award for Drama in 1984 and 1985. I've had two plays produced in the Young Playwrights Festival: *The Birthday Present* at Circle Rep in 1983 and *The Ground Zero Club,* a comedy about nuclear war, at Playwrights Horizons in 1985. At the University of Michigan I am a member of Streetlight Theater (a student-run theater group committed to producing short works by its members). I think that acting, directing, and play writing are all part of the same thing, and in Streetlight Theater I have been able to pursue them all.

About the Play

It was exciting and somewhat overwhelming to have a professional production of my play at the age of seventeen, and I was very happy to get another chance with a new play two years later. During the second, *The Ground Zero Club,* I had more of an idea of what I wanted for the production. I was able to assert myself better and disagree when I had to. I hope to continue writing for the theater and I also hope to continue writing comedy.

LIARS

by Joseph Yesutis
(age seventeen when play was written)

CHARACTERS

TOM, a second-year high-school student
ROB, a fourth-year high-school student
BRIAN, a fourth-year high-school student and a
dormitory proctor
Boys living in school dormitory

This play is dedicated to Jerry Zaks, Charles Fuller,
Bill Hart, Mark Moses, William O'Leary, and Preston Maybank for bringing *Liars* to life; and above
all, to Lane Bateman who, by teaching me his craft,
allowed the play to be written in the first place.

A typical boy's dormitory room at a present-day boarding school.

The play begins in darkness. Light enters through an opening door, and a figure can be seen entering the room. The door closes. There is a momentary pause. Heavy breathing is heard.

ROB: Who is it? *(No answer.)* Hey, who's there? *(No answer.)* You throw water on me, I swear I'll kill you. *(Silence.)* Get out of my room! I'm trying to sleep. I don't have time for this!

TOM: I think I killed myself.

ROB: Tom? Is that you? You sleeping in here again?

TOM: I didn't mean to cut it so bad.

ROB: What?

TOM: I wanted to scare my dad. Mom said don't let Dad know. God, please don't let Dad find out.

ROB: Turn on the light.

TOM: I'll be okay. My dad would think it was—

ROB: Wait a minute. I don't understand what you're saying. Turn the light on, Tom.

TOM: No, I'm all right. I'm okay. Keep the light off. I don't want you to see me. Nothing's wrong. Everything's okay.

ROB: Then tell me tomorrow! I've got Dinkerman at eight for bio, and I've gotta get some sleep!

(Loud pounding is heard from the room next door.)

VOICE: Shut up in there, huh? I gotta get some sleep, too, jerk!

ROB: All right! All right! *(Quietly.)* Tom, it's late; I'm tired. Tell me tomorrow, okay?

TOM *(rushed):* I didn't want this to happen. Honest to God, I don't wanna die. I only wanted to scare my dad so he'd know I wasn't what they would tell him I was, and my mother said—

ROB: Okay, Tom. I'll turn the light on. When I do, I'm gonna break your nose.

(Pause. ROB *gets out of bed. We hear a thud.)*

Ahhgg! Boy, Tom, this better be good, or you're gonna be seriously injured!

TOM *(rushed):* If I tell my dad it's a lie so I broke your face after I cut myself so he'll think I went sorta crazy . . .

ROB: Okay! I'm up now!

(The lights come up to reveal ROB *at the light switch. He is in underwear and looks rudely awakened. He is holding his shin.* TOM *is leaning against Rob's desk with his arm pressed against his chest. His chest is smeared with blood. He, too, is wearing underwear. On his arm is a crudely made shoelace tourniquet.* TOM *is staring at his wrist.)*

So, what's your— Tom, my God!

(ROB *limps over to* TOM.)

TOM: Don't touch it! Don't make it bleed!

ROB *(not knowing what to do):* Okay! Okay. I'll, ah — Let me. . . . Stay here; don't move. I'll get Mr. Warren. He'll call an ambulance. Tommy, you're bleeding. What happened?

TOM (*sitting on the desk chair, on top of Rob's clothes*): Don't leave!

ROB: I'll get help. Man, get up, you're on my pants. That looks bad! Put something on it!

TOM: No! I got it stopped. Don't touch it.

ROB: Okay, I won't. (*Pause.*) I'll get Mr. Warren as fast as I can.

TOM: Don't!

ROB: You've gotta get help! (*Pause.*) What happened? Did you fall?

TOM: Nothin'. I'm fine.

ROB: You're not fine, you fool!

TOM: Please don't leave! No one can know!

ROB: Tom, you don't know what you're saying. Get away from the door.

TOM: No! Ow! I didn't want to do it this bad. It hurts! Robbie, help me!

ROB: Tom, I'm here. I'm here. Now tell me what you did.

TOM: You can't tell.

ROB: You did that? To yourself?

TOM: Stay here and help me!

ROB: What do you want me to do? I can't do anything! You've gotta get a doctor! Move! (*Trying to get past* TOM.) I'll throw you out of the way.

TOM: Just leave me alone if you won't help me. (*Yelling.*) Just leave me alone!

(*Loud knocking is heard on the wall from next door.*)

VOICE: I'm not telling you again, Rob! Shut up in there!

ROB (*quietly*): Tom, I'm gonna help you. I'm gonna get someone. Now move!

TOM: No, Rob. You don't understand. I took the page. Then someone stole it. I thought you'd know by now. I shouldn't have called my mother. She said she won't tell Dad, but she will.

ROB: What page?

TOM: I know what I'm saying. And if anyone finds out, you're in as much trouble as I am.

ROB: What are you talking about?

VOICE: That's it! One more sound and I'll kick your teeth in!

ROB (*in a whisper*): Tom! Move! You need help.

TOM (*in a whisper*): No. You can't get anyone. Check your journal. You'll see. Page thirty-one is missing. Look.

(ROB *goes to find his carefully hidden journal.*)

ROB: You read my journal?

TOM: Why did you write it all down?

ROB: If you read my journal, I hope you bleed to death. You swore when I caught you in here you'd never go through my stuff again!

(ROB *can't find the journal, so in a fit of frustration he shoves everything on the desk onto the floor. He finally finds a notebook. He slams it on the desk and quickly goes through the pages. Suddenly he stops.*)

You dirty liar, where is it?

TOM: I don't know.

ROB: You don't know?

(ROB, *without thinking, grabs* TOM *and pulls him to his feet.*)

TOM: Oww!

ROB: I'm sorry! I'm sorry. You've got me crazy. Let me see.

TOM: No.

ROB: I want to see what you did.

TOM: No, you can't look at it.

ROB: Don't be a jerk. Give me your damn arm!

(TOM *lets* ROB *see his injured arm.*)

You've gotta get help. Right now. That'll never stop bleeding. It's gotta get sewn up. Why did you do this? Stupid! Stupid! Stupid!

(ROB *rushes to the dresser and gets several towels.*)

TOM: I don't wanna die, Rob.

ROB (*gently wiping the wound*): You're not gonna die. What's this thing?

TOM: I tied a shoelace around it to stop the—

ROB: You put a dirty shoelace—

TOM: It's a tourniquet. Don't worry, I know what I'm doing.

ROB: I can see that.

TOM: It's not bleeding anymore.

ROB: If that tourniquet stops the blood, how does your hand get blood?

TOM: I learned it at camp. I open it every five minutes.

ROB: Your whole hand's gonna fall off. You cut a vein. I'll bet you cut a vein. You know what that means? It won't stop bleeding until a doctor sees it. Why are you so stupid?

TOM: You're stupid! Writing all those lies!

ROB: Where's that page?

TOM: In my room. That's what I was tellin'—

ROB *(stands up in a panic):* I gotta get that page.

TOM: And clean up the blood on the door.

ROB: There's blood out there? If anybody sees blood, they'll come in here. *(Grabbing a towel and heading out the door.)* If you had a brain . . .

TOM: Oh, God, please help me.

(TOM *begins to lose control but forces himself to stay calm. Under the towel he slowly opens the tourniquet.)*

Oh, no! Ow. Ow.

(He quickly closes the tourniquet. He crosses to the desk and starts searching through the drawers.)

Jesus, please don't let this be happening.

(ROB *reenters with a wrinkled piece of paper and a bloodied, broken drinking glass.* TOM *continues his search without looking up at* ROB.)

Where's the cigarettes?

ROB: You are gonna die.

(ROB *holds out the page.*)

TOM: Where are your cigarettes?

ROB: Where's my page? This is a copy. Where's the original?

TOM: I don't have it. I mean I did, but now I don't.

ROB: You did, but now you don't?

TOM: I had it, but it's gone.

ROB: Where is it?

TOM: I don't know.

ROB: I'm not going to lift a finger till I find the original. You can bleed to death for all I care.

TOM: Rob, I don't know where it is.

ROB: Where did you get this copy?

TOM: It was stapled to the bulletin board.

ROB: Where?

TOM: The bulletin board.

ROB: Downstairs?

(TOM *nods yes.*)

This isn't happening.

TOM: Where are your cigarettes?

ROB: I don't have any!

TOM: You always have cigarettes! Now give 'em to me!

(ROB *gets up and storms over to the desk. He finds the cigarettes and throws them at* TOM *who catches them with one hand.* ROB *holds out the bloodied drinking glass.)*

ROB: You're gonna bleed to death.

TOM: I'm fine. I'm fine. *(Fumbling with the cigarettes.)* Would you help me?

(ROB *takes the cigarettes, puts one in Tom's mouth and lights it. Then* ROB *takes it back and takes a drag.)*

ROB: On the bulletin board? The whole dorm has seen that page. I don't believe this. *(Suddenly.)* What did you tell your mom?

TOM: She said she won't tell Dad— She will. He'll come up here and get me. He'll really kill me.

ROB: You shouldn't have called your parents.

TOM: When I knew people knew about your journal . . .

ROB *(hopefully):* Maybe no one saw it.

TOM: Of course people saw it. If they didn't, they will. The original's still out there. I've ruined everything.

ROB: That was the only thing you could think to do: Kill yourself?

TOM: I should've killed you! None of this would be happening if you didn't write it down.

ROB: Why did you steal it?

TOM: I thought if I took it, when you found it gone you'd say something. So I could get you to talk about it. Why did you write it? Did you ever think about what would happen if anyone saw it?

ROB: How did I know you'd steal it?

TOM: I didn't think—

ROB: So what else is new? *(Pause.)* What are my parents gonna say? We'll be thrown out!

TOM: Where's the Scotch?

ROB: Forget it.

TOM: I want some Scotch.

ROB: No!

TOM: I know where it is. Do you want me to get it?

ROB: I'm liking you less and less.

(ROB *finds the bottle. He takes a straight shot.* TOM *takes one while* ROB *lights another cigarette.)*

TOM: I know how we can get out of this.

ROB: How? My name's all over that page.

TOM: We tell them it was forged.

ROB: Give it up. No one will believe that.

TOM: They will. After we fight.

ROB: Fight?

TOM: We have to fight. Look, if we act like we had a fight, and now we hate each other, we'll be okay.

ROB: It won't work.

TOM: Yes, it will! We've gotta punch each other a couple of times. Now hit me.

ROB *(taking a shot from the bottle):* No.

TOM: Hit me.

ROB: This is stupid.

TOM: You got a better idea? *(Pause.)* If you don't

hit me, everybody is going to believe what you wrote. You've ruined my life!

ROB: Ruined your life? Everything I wrote happened! I'm the one—

TOM: You! You didn't write a thing about you; you just blamed everything on me. *(Reading paper.)* "Tom said," "Tom looked," "I think Tom is." *(Pause. Looking at* ROB.) This isn't even what happened!

ROB: It is too!

TOM: Don't lie! I was there!

ROB: What I wrote is exactly what happened.

TOM *(yelling):* You liar!

(A loud knock is heard.)

ROB: Who is it?

BRIAN: Brian.

(ROB *mouths "Damn."*)

ROB: Hold on! Just a minute!

(The knocking continues. ROB frantically waves his arms to clear the smoke. TOM clumsily hides the bottle. ROB grabs a clean towel.)

Give me your arm.

(ROB *takes the bloodied towel off Tom's arm and replaces it with a clean one. He throws the used towel under the bed.* TOM *sits on the bed as* ROB *opens the door.)*

Hey, Brian.

BRIAN: I can hear you two all the way downstairs.

ROB: Okay. Sorry. We'll be quiet.

BRIAN: Tom, you're supposed to be in your room. It's past eleven. *(Noticing underwear.)* Is that blood? Looks like you got your period.

TOM: Oh, it's—uh—

BRIAN: All right. I wanna know what's going on in here. You're both bloody, and I smell cigarettes. You having a party, or just beating the hell out of each other?

ROB: We were having a smoke.

BRIAN: I think that's a major offense. Where are the cigarettes? (ROB *gives them to him.)* Consider them confiscated. Tom, get down to your room.

TOM: No, I'm talking to Rob.

BRIAN: You get your butt down to your room now!

ROB: Come on, Brian. It's important.

BRIAN: Talk tomorrow.

(BRIAN takes TOM by the shoulder and pulls him off the bed. ROB runs to TOM.)

ROB: Leave him alone!

(The towel falls off Tom's arm.)

BRIAN: What in the—!

(TOM covers his arm. ROB helps him up.)

ROB: I said leave him alone!

BRIAN: What happened?

TOM: I cut it.

BRIAN: I'll get Mr. Warren.

(BRIAN *crosses to door.* ROB *runs after him.*)

ROB: No one's gonna say anything!

BRIAN: He's bleeding! I'm doing something!

TOM: You can't.

BRIAN: Why?

ROB: You just can't.

BRIAN: You're gonna leave him here?

TOM: It's okay.

BRIAN: No, it's not. I'm getting Warren.

ROB *(handing* BRIAN *the journal entry):* You can't say anything.

TOM: Rob, what are you doing?

BRIAN: What's this?

ROB *(to* TOM): If he hasn't seen it, he'll hear about it.

TOM: Are you crazy?

ROB *(to* TOM): Maybe he knows who wrote it.

BRIAN: Mellow out, Tom, huh? *(Reading.)* "I came back from class and found—"

ROB: Do you have to read it out loud?

(BRIAN *reads silently, then he looks at* TOM.)

TOM *(mutters):* It's not true.

BRIAN: "We started talking about homosexuality. I think Tom is gay." Why did you show this to me?

TOM: It was stapled on the bulletin board.

BRIAN: What bulletin board?

TOM: The one downstairs.

BRIAN: The dorm bulletin board?

TOM: Yes!

ROB: You would have heard about it. Brian, none of it is true, so you can't say anything to anyone, okay?

TOM: Yeah, we don't know who wrote it. I thought Rob wrote it; he thought I wrote it. I was so mad, I did this. *(Holds out his arm.)* It's really not as bad as it looks. But we've decided to let the whole thing slide, so don't say anything, okay?

BRIAN: Bull. *(Pause. He looks at* ROB, *then at* TOM.) I won't say anything.

ROB: Promise.

BRIAN *(handing the page to* TOM): Yeah.

TOM: Good.

BRIAN: Except maybe Steve.

TOM: I knew it.

BRIAN: Steve's a proctor too. We tell each other everything. But don't worry, Steve won't say anything. I trust him.

ROB: Yeah, right, and how many friends does he have that he trusts. I know exactly what will happen.

TOM: Brian, if you say one word about this to anyone, I'm going to let everyone know you lust after Rob.

BRIAN: What?

ROB: What?

TOM: I saw you come in Rob's room while he was asleep and stare at him.

BRIAN: I never did anything like that!

TOM: I saw you stand right there and stare at him until his alarm went off.

BRIAN: It never happened!

TOM: You going to say anything to Steve?

BRIAN *(stares at* TOM, *then speaks):* No. *(Turns to go.)* I hope your arm rots!

*(*BRIAN *exits.)*

TOM: Nice move!

ROB: What?

TOM: Why did you show it to him?

ROB: It shut him up. *(Pause.)* Did he really come in here?

TOM: Right before you found me.

(Lights up momentarily to reveal the same room with the door ajar. ROB *is sleeping facedown on his bed; he is in his underwear. Enter* TOM. *He sneaks to Rob's desk and opens drawers. He finds a magazine and starts to glance through it quickly.* BRIAN *offstage, calls out from the hallway.)*

BRIAN: Rob!

*(*TOM *panics and stands close to the wall by the closet, attempting to hide.* BRIAN *enters.)*

Rob.

(He stops when he sees ROB *asleep.* BRIAN *steps out of the room and looks up and down the hallway.* TOM

desperately jams himself into the closet. The door will not quite close. BRIAN *reenters, quietly closing the door behind him. He stands at the foot of Rob's bed and studies* ROB *with great interest. Suddenly an alarm clock goes off on the desk.* BRIAN *leaves the room hurriedly.* ROB *wakes. He crosses to the desk to turn off the alarm. Then he crosses to the closet, opens the door, and jumps back.)*

ROB: What the—

TOM: I was . . . Uh—

ROB: Get out of there! Look at my things all over. . . . How long have you been in here? You just walk in anywhere you want! You are unbeliev—

TOM: I was looking for you.

ROB: In my closet? You're a damn liar!

TOM: I was looking for—

ROB: Get out. Now! I could get you in so much trouble. This is my room. Private room. So get out before— Get out!

TOM: You queer?

(ROB *hits* TOM *in the face.* ROB *finds his pants.)*

ROB: I'm turning you in. I'm gonna nail you for this one. This is my property. I hope I broke it!

TOM: You are.

ROB: I'm not wasting my time!

TOM: Yes or no?

ROB *(deliberately looking* TOM *in the face):* No.

TOM *(producing the magazine he found,* Playgirl): Liar.

ROB *(keeping his composure):* It's a prop. I used it in a play. It was a joke. A dumb joke. When I did the variety show at Christmas. I can turn you in to the faculty for going through my things. You ever hear of privacy?

TOM: Christmas was months ago.

ROB: I didn't get around to throwing it out. I forgot I had it. I'm gonna be late to class. I forgot I had it.

TOM: Liar.

ROB: I don't care what you believe! What right have you got going through my stuff?

TOM: Somebody said you had a fag mag, so I—

ROB: Who said I had a fag mag?

TOM: It doesn't matter.

ROB: Yes, it does! Who said it?

TOM: I forgot. It doesn't matter anyway.

ROB: It does matter!

TOM: What does it matter if it's not your *Playgirl?*

ROB *(grabbing the magazine and throwing it into his wastebasket):* There! Does that make you feel better? *(Grabbing* TOM.) If I ever catch you going through my things again, I'll beat you senseless! Got me? Now get out of here!

TOM *(crossing to door, then stopping):* Rob, I'm sorry. I promise I won't do that ever again. Okay? *(Pause.)* I don't care about the magazine. *(Pause.)* It doesn't mean anything. *(Pause.)* Ya know?

ROB: Yeah, I know. *(Pause.)* Go to hell!

TOM: It doesn't mean anything if you just look. *(Pause.)* It's not like you reached out and grabbed a guy.

ROB: I never grabbed anyone. I have no desire to.

TOM: Me either. *(Pause.* TOM *moves to the bed and sits.)* You ever been kissed?

ROB: What?

TOM: Nothing. It was dumb.

ROB: What'd you say?

TOM: Forget it.

ROB *(after a pause)*: No, what did you say? I ever been kissed? *(Pause.)* You mean by a guy?

TOM: Yeah.

ROB *(deliberately)*: No! *(Pause.)* You?

TOM *(forced laugh)*: Once. *(Pause.)* It wasn't a real kiss. It was an almost kiss. Last vacation. I was at a New Year's party. Everybody was drunk. It was time for the countdown; everybody staggered to the TV. We had horns, and we were all making a lot of noise. After the countdown, everybody started kissing everybody. A guy I knew for years came up . . . *(Pause.)* He kissed me. *(Pause.)* I didn't think he knew what he was doing; he was stoned out of his mind. I walked away from him. We talked later. *(He looks at* ROB.) I told him I wasn't interested.

ROB: Something like that happened to me too.

TOM: You said you'd never been kissed.

ROB: He kissed me. I didn't kiss him. There's a difference.

TOM: Well?

ROB: Well what?

TOM: I told you.

ROB *(after a pause):* I was at camp two years ago. Everyone in my cabin went on a hike. One of those outdoor challenge things where everyone has to work together to get through the forest. The first night out, after we ate and pitched the tents and stuff, me and about four other guys got together in one of the tents to play cards. I think we were drunk. Yeah, we were drunk. After a couple of hands someone wanted to play strip poker. We played awhile. We're all sitting in our underwear. *(Pause.)* The other guys got tired and took their clothes back to their tents. Just me and this other kid were left. He wanted to play one more hand. *(Laughs.)* He lost. *(Pause.)* Then he—he leaned over and kissed me. I didn't do nothin'. Next day, he was embarrassed. He didn't look at me or talk to me. *(Pause.)* I guess he thought I was going to say something.

TOM: You embarrassed?

ROB: No. Didn't bother me. I don't care what people do.

TOM: That kind of thing doesn't bother me either. *(Long pause.)* What are you thinking about now?

ROB: Nothing.

TOM: Liar. Come on, what you thinking about?

ROB: No comment.

TOM: Tell me.

ROB: You don't want to know.

TOM: Do you want— Forget it.

ROB: What?

TOM *(apprehensive):* Do you wanna try kissing me?

ROB: No.

TOM: You sure?

(ROB *doesn't respond.* TOM *touches Rob's face.* ROB *closes his eyes.* TOM *draws nearer, preparing to give* ROB *a kiss.* ROB *draws away, not looking at* TOM.)

ROB: I think you better go now.

(TOM *remains motionless for a moment, then turns and crosses to the door, silently. He leaves the room. As the door closes, lights out. Lights up again to reveal the room as it was before the flashback.* TOM *and* ROB *are standing near the desk staring at each other.)*

I'm sorry that ever happened.

TOM: I'm not. I don't mind what happened.

ROB: I do. And you should too. That never should've happened.

TOM: Right. *(Pause.)* Just break my nose. (TOM *closes his eyes, waiting.)*

ROB: It's a dumb plan. You saw how well Brian bought it.

TOM *(quietly):* Rob.

ROB: It won't work.

TOM: I can't move my hand!

ROB: Let me see.

TOM: I can't feel it, Robbie. I can't feel it!

ROB: It's bad. Please. You gotta see someone. Now. I thought you were keeping an eye on it! What happened to your tourniquet? Didn't you open it every five minutes?

TOM: When you went to my room I opened it, but it bled again!

ROB: I'm getting you to the hospital.

TOM: We can't. They'll find out! They'll call my parents! Your parents too!

ROB (*pulling* TOM *toward the door*): I don't care anymore!

TOM: Let's do the plan! Please.

ROB: No!

TOM: What are you going to tell them when they find out you're gay? (ROB *stops.*) You got any better ideas?

ROB: I'm not gay!

TOM: I know, I know. So hit me! (*Pause.*) Hurry! My arm hurts!

ROB (*helplessly*): I can't. Not with your arm like that. You hit me.

TOM: Okay. (*He tries to hit* ROB *but doesn't want to take the free hand away from his wrist.*) I can't. It'll start bleeding. You have to hit me!

(ROB *draws back to hit* TOM.)

ROB: I can't.

TOM (*in a stage whisper, goading*): Come on, sissy. You can do it! (ROB *looks at him motionless.*) Faggot. You are a faggot. Rob the fag.

(ROB *gets angry, to the point of almost hitting* TOM. TOM *sees that* ROB *won't hit him, so he crosses to the closet and pulls out the* Playgirl *magazine from the flashback.* TOM *holds the magazine out to* ROB.)

Faggot.

(ROB *draws back as if to hit* TOM, *but instead he moves in suddenly, and they kiss. As soon as they touch lips, the door opens and* BRIAN *enters. Other boys can be seen in the open doorway.*)

BRIAN: Tom— (*He sees the two boys, who immediately separate, and looks at them a moment, smiling.*) Tom, your dad's on the phone with Mr. Warren. They would like a word with you. Now.

(*Exit* BRIAN, *closing the door. Muted laughter can be heard from outside the door.*)

TOM: Rob.
ROB: Please don't.
TOM: I love you.
ROB: I don't want to hear this.
TOM: I can't help it. I do. I love you.
ROB (*knocking* TOM *to the floor*): Shut up, you queer!
VOICE: They're having a lovers' quarrel.
VOICE: Lock your doors tonight!
VOICE: Let's throw 'em in the river!
BRIAN: Homos on the floor! Everyone zip up!

(Laughter and insults continue as the boys in the hall walk away. TOM *sits up on the floor as* ROB *sits on the bed. Neither boy looks at the other.* TOM *tries to untie the shoelace. His hand is now painfully swollen.)*

TOM: Ow! *(He tries again, then gives up, cradling his arm.)*

ROB *(forces a laugh):* Aren't you dead yet?

TOM: I should be so lucky.

ROB: You better go talk to your dad. Hand looks bad.

TOM *(moving to door):* I'm sure every guy in the dorm knows by now.

ROB: Your dad will probably come up here.

TOM: Can I hide in your closet?

ROB: I'll go talk to Mr. Warren and your dad with you. Okay?

TOM: You don't have to. It's all my fault. I'll deal with it. *(He starts to leave.)* My arm really hurts. You think Brian's told my dad yet? *(Pause.)* What he saw?

ROB: Forget about Brian!

TOM: Sure.

ROB: If all I mean to my friends doesn't mean anything to my friends, who needs 'em?

TOM: You'll really come talk . . . to my dad with me?

ROB: Your dad's okay.

TOM: He won't be.

ROB: He love you?

TOM: Yeah. Yeah, he does.

ROB: Okay then. You love him?

TOM: Yeah. *(Fast.)* I love you too.

ROB: Don't tell your dad that.

TOM: You could still break my nose.

ROB: You gotta get fixed up enough already. They'll probably cut it off.

TOM *(laughing):* Oww! That's not funny.

ROB: Just don't tell your dad what you said.

TOM: But I do love you.

ROB: You can't be that dumb.

TOM: I don't care. *(Pause as they look at each other.)* I don't care!

ROB: It's not fair.

TOM: I DON'T CARE!

(They exit.)

THE END

JOSEPH YESUTIS

I was born in Chicago and grew up in Burr Ridge, Illinois, a suburb outside the city. I attended Phillips Exeter Academy for four years and will be a freshman at Harvard in the fall, where I hope to continue my study of play writing.

About the Play

Plays are not written. Plays are rewritten. Again and again. Finally, three years after I unwittingly enrolled in my first play-writing course, I have accepted that fundamental truth about play writing. Like most beginning writers, I just wanted to write my plays and not waste time studying plot development or character analysis. I vividly remember typing the first draft of *Liars* the night before it was due. Any word that entered my head hit the page; I was an artist experiencing divine inspiration. That notion quickly vanished, however, after the first humbling D+, and I allowed myself to be taught that there was more to it. Printed here is the twelfth version of *Liars*—by no means finished, but merely abandoned. To some people, twelve complete rewrites may not seem worth the effort, but I understand that publication after twelve drafts is a gift from God. Most important, of course, is that it was produced, and that makes any amount of work worthwhile. Watching two years of work on paper come alive for thirty minutes on stage was the most gratifying experience of my life. Being a finalist in the competition, or strutting down the streets of New York City for a week as a semicelebrity, became meaningless after I watched my work being respected and enjoyed by an audience.

My advice to any beginning writer is the same great advice Charles Fuller gave me in New York. Write everyday, read everything you can get your hands on, and learn the basic play-writing techniques. It's safe to assume that the people who write those texts aren't filling them with fundamental theater concepts for lack of something better to do. If you want to be a playwright, take time to learn how plays are written.

TENDER PLACES

by Jason Brown
(age twelve when play was written)

CHARACTERS

Paul, Eric's father
Mary, Eric's mother
Eric, a twelve-year-old boy
Sam, an old woman in the park

Scene One

MARY's *living room.*

A hallway can be seen stage right. Lights up as a doorbell starts ringing. We hear, but do not see, MARY run from hallway to the door. She backs onto stage as PAUL barges in.

PAUL: I'd like to have Eric for the weekend.

MARY: And hello to you, Paul . . . just barge right in.

PAUL: It's my house too.

MARY: We've been over this before. I'm trying to get the money for your half.

(PAUL looks around the room. He picks up mail and looks through it.)

PAUL: Well, until that time . . .

MARY *(angry):* It would help if you sent the support payments on time.

PAUL: Do I get Eric or not?

(ERIC enters from the hall. He's anxious.)

ERIC: Hi, Dad.

MARY: Eric! Go to your room for a minute. Your father and I have some things to talk about.

ERIC: But I didn't do anything!

PAUL: Hey, Eric. I got tickets for the Steeler-Cowboy game on Saturday!

ERIC: ALL RIGHT!

MARY: Wait a minute! That's a dirty trick. This is MY time with Eric.

ERIC *(starts to pout):* OH . . . MOM!

MARY: We're supposed to visit the Hammers' farm.

ERIC: Yeah . . . but THE STEELERS! You can have me extra next week . . . okay?

MARY: Go get some clean clothes.

ERIC *(begins to exit):* ALL RIGHT!

(MARY turns on PAUL and continues fighting.)

MARY: That was rotten.

PAUL: Just trying to make the kid happy.

MARY: You make it sound like I don't.

PAUL: If you wanted him happy, we'd still be married.

MARY: You honestly believe it's all my fault.

PAUL: Look, I just wanna take the kid to a game. Why do you always start?

MARY: ME? From here on we stick to the schedule.

PAUL: Nobody tells me when I can see my kid. Not YOU . . . your boyfriend—

MARY: THE JUDGE! He made a schedule.

PAUL: The schedule's gonna be changed.

(Enter ERIC with an overnight bag. His parents do not know that he is listening.)

MARY: What do you mean?

PAUL: I think Eric should live with me.

MARY: Over my dead body!

PAUL: A boy needs his father.

MARY *(sarcastically):* He doesn't need his mother?

PAUL: Hey, you're gonna marry that jerk . . . you have each other. I filed for custody.

MARY: WHAT???

PAUL: Why should I be a part-time father?

MARY: Why should I be a part-time mother?

(ERIC walks over to stand between them.)

ERIC: Why should I be a part-time kid?

(PAUL and MARY are startled. MARY kneels and holds ERIC.)

MARY: OH, BABY!

PAUL: He's not a baby.

(PAUL takes one of Eric's arms. MARY takes the other. The boy is pulled between them.)

ERIC: AWW . . . come on!

PAUL: Eric, next week the judge wants to talk with you.

ERIC: ME? What for?

PAUL: He wants to ask you some questions.

MARY: PAUL. . . .

ERIC: Am I really gonna live with you, Dad?

MARY: NO!

PAUL: If that's what you want.

MARY: You don't want that . . . do you?

ERIC: I don't know.

PAUL: Don't we always have fun together?

ERIC: I guess so. . . .

MARY *(frantic):* Fun isn't everything. It's taking care of you. I don't have time to have fun with you —OH!

(ERIC lowers his head.)

But I want to—I want to have fun with you.

(ERIC pulls away from them.)

PAUL: Come on, champ, we'll talk about this later.

MARY: You can't do this. *(MARY follows them to the door.)* Eric. I'll call you tonight. . . . Okay . . . baby?

ERIC: I'm not a baby. Good-bye . . . Mom.

BLACKOUT

Scene Two

PAUL's *apartment.*

The next day. It's late. ERIC *is sitting with a shopping bag full of toys.* PAUL *is exhausted.*

ERIC: Hey, Dad! That purple monster that ate Brooklyn was neat.

PAUL: You've seen it seven times in the past month.

ERIC: I wanna go again tomorrow.

PAUL: You gotta be kidding!

ERIC: You said I could do anything.

PAUL: Yeah, but . . . come on!

ERIC: That's okay . . . Mom'll take me.

PAUL: NO . . . NO! We'll go again. No problem.
ERIC: Well . . . I dunno. Maybe . . .

(PAUL is silent; he looks angry.)

Maybe we'll see that one about the giant bean. (Snootily.) Don't get too excited about it, Dad. Mom'll take me.
PAUL: Okay . . . Okay. We'll go.
ERIC: How about . . . a home computer?
PAUL *(looking in the bag):* Look at all these—figures . . . comic books . . .
ERIC: I want . . . something else.
PAUL: These'll keep you busy for a year!

(ERIC kicks the bag and, sulking, sits in the chair.)

What more do you want?
ERIC: I want to go to another game tomorrow.
PAUL: What?
ERIC: The Steeler-Cowboys. Are we going?
PAUL: Look, Eric, this isn't like you.

(ERIC sulks.)

Hey, kiddo. What is it? You mad at me?

(No answer.)

Hey . . . ya know . . . if you come to live with me . . . know what we're gonna get?
ERIC: What?
PAUL: A DOG!

ERIC *(scared):* A dog? NO! *(Starts to yell.)* I DON'T WANT A DOG!

PAUL: What do you mean? You've always wanted a dog! Your mother wouldn't let you have one!

ERIC: 'Cause she's allergic to them.

PAUL: Well, I'm not. So if you live with me . . . we'll get one.

ERIC: NO!

PAUL: Eric . . .

ERIC: Maybe I'm allergic too! Maybe it'll get killed by a car! *(ERIC is really upset.)* Maybe it'll run away!

PAUL: STOP IT! What's the matter with you?

ERIC: I don't want anything! I don't! Hear me?

PAUL *(angry):* You sure wanted a lot today, kiddo. I gave you a lot.

ERIC: Not what I really want.

(ERIC kicks the toys.)

PAUL: You're acting like a brat. That's not like you—

ERIC: Dad . . .

PAUL: I try to give you what you want but it's never enough—

ERIC: But . . . Dad!

PAUL: Try thinking about me for a change.

ERIC: I CAN'T!

PAUL: What do you mean you can't?

(Silence.)

I love you. That's why I do all this.

ERIC: Mom says she loves me, too, and that's why she DOESN'T buy me a lot of toys. She says you're trying to bribe me.

PAUL: She never knew when to shut up. That's one of the reasons I left her.

ERIC: What are the other reasons?

PAUL: That's none of your business, Son.

ERIC: She said you had a girlfriend.

PAUL: That's enough, Eric.

ERIC: Is it true? *(Excited.)* She said she was sorry she wasted all those years with you.

PAUL: You're just like her . . . you don't know when to shut up!

ERIC: Are you going to leave me too?

PAUL: Of course not! I love you, Eric.

ERIC: Ya know, I get tired of people loving me so much.

PAUL: Should we hate you?

ERIC: Yeah! Maybe it wouldn't hurt as much.

BLACKOUT

Scene Three

MARY's *apartment.*

The next day. ERIC *is sitting in a chair; he is unhappy.*

MARY: So, did you have a good time with your father?

ERIC: Yeah.

MARY: Boy, you sound cheerful.

ERIC: Look, Ma, I'm busy. What do you want?

MARY: Busy? Doing what? *(Silence.)* We have to talk. *(Nervous.)* You know, Bill and I have been going together for a year now . . . and, uh, this custody thing and all— Bill and I thought . . .

ERIC: Yeah?

MARY: You're not making this easy. Well, we thought . . . two things—

ERIC: What do you want?

MARY: To give you a good home. Bill and I are getting married.

ERIC: Don't do me any favors.

MARY: You like Bill . . . and someday, maybe, you'll love him like I do.

ERIC: Why bother? He'll just go away someday too.

MARY: We want what's best for you. I love you.

ERIC: Is Bill gonna tell me that too?

MARY: Well, I hope so.

ERIC: At least you didn't offer me a dog.

MARY: Don't be smart, Eric.

ERIC (*sarcastically*): Don't be smart, Eric; don't be dumb, Eric. Don't be sad, Eric. Grow up . . . you're too young, act your age—you're making me crazy!

MARY: Eric, we want you to see a counselor . . . psychologist.

ERIC: Oh, no! You make me nuts, then I go to the shrink? WHY DON'T YOU GO? AND DAD? AND BILL? DON'T FORGET DAD'S GIRL-FRIEND!

MARY: I don't think you're crazy, Eric. I do think you're confused and need help sorting this out. I want you to be happy.

ERIC (*pleading*): Look, Ma. It's not too late! You and Dad—

MARY: STOP IT!

ERIC: —can make up. We can be a family again—

MARY: Be serious.

ERIC: I don't even care about the dog.

MARY: It can't happen . . . ever.

ERIC: You don't care. If you did, you'd try some more.

MARY: I do care. . . . I tried . . . real hard. It just didn't work. It'll never work. I had to leave him so I could be happy.

ERIC: Now you're happy! Great! That's all that matters, Mom. It's not fair.

MARY: You can be happy, too, if you want it. I can't give you any guarantees, Eric.

ERIC: I was happy before.

MARY: Give it a chance. Try to understand.

ERIC: I understand! You and Dad fell out of love, I have to choose one of you. You throw in an extra father just to make it more interesting . . . and you expect me to be happy. I'M NOT! So . . . the kid's nuts. Yeah, I understand.

BLACKOUT

Scene Four

A park.

  The next day. Enter ERIC *stage left.* SAM, *an old bag lady, is sitting on a bench.* ERIC *is walking slowly with his head hanging.* SAM *watches* ERIC *and as he passes the bench, she calls to him.*

SAM: Hello.

ERIC *(pauses and turns to SAM):* Hi.

SAM: What's your name?

ERIC: Eric. *(ERIC begins to walk again.)*

SAM: Just call me . . . uhh . . . Sam.

(ERIC turns back again. Silence. He hangs his head.)

What's wrong?

ERIC: Nothing.

SAM: Something is.

(ERIC goes and sits next to Sam.)

ERIC: How do you know?

SAM: I had a son.

ERIC: Had? What happened to him?

SAM: He died.

(ERIC begins to cry.)

Whoa! Slow down. Why are you crying?

ERIC: Because everyone I love seems to die. Not really die . . . but it seems like it.

SAM: Here today . . . gone tomorrow. I been around a long time. Know what you mean.

ERIC: How old— How long you been around?

SAM *(hand on her chin and looking up):* I probably know, but I forgot.

ERIC: YOU FORGOT?

SAM: Sooo . . . what do you study in school?

ERIC: Which one?

SAM: Which one? How many you go to?

ERIC *(counting on his fingers):* The Progressive School for Gifted Children, Art Institute for the Exceptionally Gifted, Middle Scholars Program. Saturdays are for the private lessons in music and body movement—

SAM: Wait a minute, there. How come you go to so many schools?

ERIC: I'm a gifted child.

SAM: If you're so gifted, why do you go to school to learn how to move your body?

ERIC: Pardon me?

SAM: How old are you?

ERIC: Twelve.

SAM: You want a cookie?

ERIC (backing away): No, thanks.

SAM: So, what's your problem?

ERIC: My parents are divorced. I'm getting a stepfather and they think I'm crazy, so they're sending me to a shrink.

SAM: Are you crazy?

ERIC: 'Course not. But they are. Why do I need another father?

SAM: Why does he need another son?

ERIC: He doesn't have kids. I kinda wish he did. They could argue over someone else for a while.

SAM: Do you think that's all they do? Argue over you?

ERIC: Yeah. Now I have to choose who I want to live with.

SAM: Oh . . . I see. Choose between your father and your mother and old what's-his-name.

ERIC: Bill. He's okay, I guess . . . but he's not going to be my father. I have a perfectly good one. Well, most of the time.

SAM: What about grandmothers? You got any of those?

ERIC: I never knew them.

SAM: How about me? Want me for a grandmother?

ERIC: You can't do that—just become my grandmother. It doesn't work that way.

SAM: Oh, I see. You're one for following the rules by the book.

ERIC: Why do I need a grandmother? They just die, anyhow.

SAM: Why do I need a grandson? They just grow up and lead their own lives. So . . . Mr. Smart Guy. You have a perfectly good father and no need of anything called a stepfather . . . or grandmother. Suits me just fine too!

ERIC: I'm sorry, I didn't mean to make you mad.

SAM: Do you have a dog?

ERIC *(startled):* No. *(Slight pause.)* Why?

SAM: Why not?

ERIC: I never wanted one.

SAM *(yelling):* WHY NOT?

ERIC: I never wanted one. WHY ARE YOU YELLING AT ME?

SAM: Tell me why no dog . . . no grandmother . . . no one else allowed in your life, smarty-pants. TELL ME!

ERIC *(crying):* BECAUSE THEY'LL GO AWAY!

They'll all go away, anyhow. And you'll just die—
I'll start to love you and you'll die and go away too.

SAM *(gently):* I see . . . Mr. Smarty-Pants.

ERIC: Don't call me that.

SAM: Why not? You think you know everything.
You don't even know THE MOST IMPORTANT
THING . . . ever.

ERIC: What?

SAM: You think I can just sit on this bench and just
tell you THE MOST IMPORTANT THING
EVER? You think that's how it happens?

ERIC: Are you teasing me?

SAM: Would I . . . your unwanted grandmother-
to-be . . . tease you?

ERIC: Then tell me.

SAM: I don't have to. You just told yourself.

ERIC: WHAT?

SAM: Well, let's see. *(Slight pause.)* You just said
. . . people don't always love each other . . . for-
ever. Right?

ERIC: Well, yeah.

SAM: And sometimes other people have to choose.
They're put in the middle . . . right?

ERIC: Yeah.

SAM: And sometimes they even die. The ones you
love. Is that right?

ERIC: SO?

SAM: So . . . maybe it's better not to EVER love
ANYTHING. Yes?

ERIC: Well . . .

SAM: And that way you can't ever feel ANY-THING. HAPPY . . . SAD . . . CRAZY. You just can't feel.

ERIC: Well, no . . . it's just not fair!

SAM: That's most important. I bet . . . YOU'RE ALWAYS FAIR.

(Silence.)

And they REALLY don't love you. Do you think? *(Pause.)* They really love you?

ERIC: Yeah . . . they do . . . but—

SAM: And old . . . what's-his-name. He CAN'T LOVE YOU. Right?

ERIC: No, Bill's okay. He really is.

SAM: But the dog. He'd just have to run away. I understand that.

ERIC: Not really. I mean, I want a dog . . . but what if it dies?

SAM: I can guarantee that it will.

ERIC: SEE!

SAM: 'Course, you'd miss all of the happy years in between his dying.

ERIC: Maybe he won't die for a long time.

SAM: And those parents of yours. They don't deserve you. They must be pretty selfish.

ERIC: No, they're good. They love me.

SAM: Don't be too sure.

ERIC *(angry):* I know they do. Even my dad. He's not always there, but I know he loves me.

SAM: What about making you choose. That's love?

ERIC: Dad's just mad and hurt 'cause Mom and Bill are getting married.

SAM: I don't know. *(Pause.)* They should just spend their lives making YOU happy.

ERIC: When Mom and Dad are happy . . . themselves . . . it's always better. Hey! It really doesn't have anything to do with me.

SAM: Ya don't say.

ERIC: I got to go home now.

(Excited, ERIC starts to walk offstage. SAM exits without ERIC seeing her. ERIC turns back to SAM and sees the empty bench.)

SAM? SAM?

(ERIC is sad. He walks to the bench and runs his hand over the back of it. He sees the cookie bag and takes a cookie. He starts to laugh.)

HEY, SAM. *(Pause.)* I'm gonna get a dog. A DOG, SAM. A REAL BIG ONE.

(ERIC exits.)

BLACKOUT

JASON BROWN

I was born on April 9, 1971. I live in Pittsburgh, Pennsylvania, in a section called Regent Square. I am now fourteen years old, and I am in the eighth grade at Reizenstein Middle School. I have many interests besides writing. I've been acting since I was three years old; I collect comic books and coins; and I'm interested in drawing and photography. I play the guitar and piano, and I'm in the school band, in the media club, and on the yearbook staff. I live with my mother and stepfather, Carol and Jeffrey Cohen, my brother, Justin (eleven), and stepbrothers, Michael (fifteen) and Joshua (twelve) Cohen, along with assorted dogs, cats, hermit crabs, and snakes. My life is busy, interesting, and fun.

About the Play

I entered the Young Playwrights Festival on a dare from my mother. She's a writer and encouraged my brothers and me to write a play. I never dreamed that my play, *Tender Places,* would do so well. I received rave reviews from the New York critics and was interviewed by many papers, magazines, and television people. It was great! I had a lot of fun. My play was just purchased by Group W Westinghouse, and it's being made into a national television special. I hope to continue in the theater, writing, acting, and directing. The Festival experience was wonderful. The people treated me as an equal and respected my writing, a rare experience for a thirteen-year-old. It also taught me that you should try to get what you want; no matter what your age, it just may happen.

A NEW APPROACH TO HUMAN SACRIFICE

by Peter Getty
(age sixteen when play was written)

CHARACTERS

MRS. WALL
MR. WALL
BOBBY WALL, eight years old
MICHAEL WALL, sixteen years old
SUSAN WALL, fifteen years old
ALVIN, Susan's date

The Walls' living room.

An evening in late spring.

Lights come up to reveal stage, the surrealistically happy suburban home of the Wall family.

MRS. WALL *is cleaning. She sprays the room with air freshener, and carries with her a feather duster and a basket full of brightly-colored cleaning products. She is perky and sunshiny to a degree that suggests mania.*

MR. WALL *is seated in an easy chair, his face hidden behind the newspaper he is reading; he is smoking a pipe.*

BOBBY *sits either in his father's lap or against his feet —preferably the former—watching TV. He is inert. The TV is faintly audible throughout the play. Cartoon music would be good.*

The phone rings. MRS. WALL *looks at it, confused, tries for a time to ignore it, and then answers it.*

MRS. WALL: Good evening, this is the Wall residence. May I help you? . . . Yes, I think he's in. Just a moment, please. *(Calling off.)* Michael! Phone call for you!

*(*MICHAEL *enters from whichever side it was toward which she didn't call, takes the phone from her hand, and sits on a couch.* MRS. WALL *returns to her cleaning.)*

MICHAEL: Hey, Clarisse, how'd it go? . . . Oh, you won't know until it gets back. . . . Gosh, I guess you might. Anyway, why should he care? . . . I don't know—a coat hanger, knitting needles, an eggbeater, whatever. . . . Why, what's the problem?

MRS. WALL *(to* MR. WALL): Honey? *(Pause.)* Honey?

MR. WALL: Mm?

MRS. WALL: Honey, I—I'm worried about Susan's date tonight.

MR. WALL: Mm.

MRS. WALL: You know, he seems a nice enough boy and all that, but . . . I'm not sure he's really Susie's *type.*

MR. WALL: Ah.

(There is a beeping noise. MRS. WALL *looks down at her watch.)*

MRS. WALL: Eight o'clock, Bobby; time for bed.

MR. WALL *(to* BOBBY, *without coming from behind the paper): * Hear that, sport?

(MR. WALL *pats him affectionately on the head.* BOBBY *doesn't so much as budge.)*

Now, hustle off to bed. *(Pause.* MR. WALL *calls off.)* And don't forget to brush your teeth.

(Pause. MR. WALL *looks out from behind the paper and addresses the audience in a tone of warm, fatherly pride.)*

That son of mine.

MICHAEL: I bet that should show you how easy it's

getting. . . . But why do they all call her "tarpaulin"? . . . Yeah, well, I guess that's why they use carrot sticks, honey. . . . Well, yes, assuming he can read braille . . .

MRS. WALL: Honey?

MR. WALL: Mm?

MRS. WALL *(confused):* I *was* saying something to you earlier, wasn't I?

MR. WALL: Something?

MRS. WALL: About . . . Susan!

MR. WALL: Yes?

MRS. WALL: Honey, how do you feel about that boy Susie's going to the prom with?

MR. WALL: Well. Boy. *(Pause.)* We've talked that stuff over with her, haven't we?

MRS. WALL: No.

(Pause.)

MR. WALL: Well. *(Pause.)* He's a nice boy, isn't he, her date?

MRS. WALL: Who?

MR. WALL: Well, this boy who's taking little Susie to the prom.

MRS. WALL: Alvin?

MR. WALL: Well, is that his name?

MRS. WALL: Whose?

MR. WALL: Well . . . her date's.

MRS. WALL: Yes.

MR. WALL: Well, is he a nice boy?

MRS. WALL: That's what I wanted to talk to you about.

MR. WALL: What?

MRS. WALL: Alvin.

MR. WALL: Alvin. Say, would that be the Alvin Susie is going out with?

MRS. WALL: Yes.

MR. WALL: Mm.

MRS. WALL: Well, what do you think of him, honey?

MR. WALL: I can't say I've ever met the boy.

MRS. WALL: We can't just let little Susie go to the senior prom with someone we don't even know!

MR. WALL: Well, how long have they been going out?

MRS. WALL: I don't know.

MR. WALL: *Are* they going out?

MRS. WALL: I don't know.

MR. WALL: Well, what time is he picking her up?

MRS. WALL: Eight-thirty. He's picking her up at eight-thirty.

MR. WALL: Well, let's speak with Susan about him.

MRS. WALL: Yes, let's do that.

(They smile.)

MR. WALL: Well.

(MRS. WALL *returns to her housework,* MR. WALL *to his newspaper. Enter* SUSAN *in an evening dress. This is her first night in high heels, and she bursts in with an awkward flourish in the course of which she nearly falls. She stops in front of her father, curtsies clumsily, smiles widely—exposing a mouthful of gleaming silver braces—and emits a high-pitched, nasal giggle. She is hideous.* MR. *and* MRS. WALL *beam.)*

SUSAN: How do I look, Daddy?

MR. WALL: Like my little princess.

SUSAN: Oh, Daddy.

(MR. *and* MRS. WALL *exchange nervous glances.)*

MR. WALL (*addresses* SUSAN *in a fatherly tone):* Now, Susan, your mother and I were wondering if you could tell us something about this boy coming over this evening.

SUSAN *(taken a little aback):* I guess he's a nice boy.

(MR. *and* MRS. WALL *beam at each other and return to their activities.)*

He's sort of . . . different.

(MR. *and* MRS. WALL *suddenly stare at* SUSAN, *shocked.)*

MR. WALL: Different?

SUSAN: I don't know, he's—he's not exactly the same.

(MR. *and* MRS. WALL *look at each other, aghast.)*

MICHAEL: So why doesn't she get it replaced? . . .
I know, but he won't be either. . . . Uh-huh. . . .
No, none anywhere. . . . No, I hear that doesn't
work all that well . . .

(MR. *and* MRS. WALL *return to their activities.* SU-
SAN *goes and sits on the couch next to* MICHAEL. *She
fidgets nervously, pats her hair, checks herself in a
makeup mirror.*)

MRS. WALL: You know, you're sitting where Bobby
spilled that macaroni and cheese.

(SUSAN *leaps to her feet, panic-stricken.*)

Oh. No. I guess that wasn't it. Sorry, sweety.

(SUSAN *sits back down shakily.*)

MICHAEL: No, no, Shannon's terrific. . . . But
didn't it begin to hurt after a while?
SUSAN *(to her mother):* Is it eight-thirty yet?
MRS. WALL *(blissfully):* Hm?
SUSAN: What time is it, Mom?

(MRS. WALL *jerks up from whatever it is she was
cleaning; she is holding a wad of chewed gum.*)

MRS. WALL *(angrily):* All right, everyone, who's
been putting gum on the furniture?
MICHAEL *(cupping a hand over the receiver):* It was
Bobby. He's been putting gum all over everything,
ever since he saw Captain Kill do it on TV.

MR. WALL: Well, the Bruins beat the White Sox in overtime, four to three.

SUSAN: Mom? Is my hair all right?

MICHAEL: Listen, I never even heard of that kind of cereal . . .

MRS. WALL: Bobby, have you been putting gum on the furniture?

MR. WALL: The Contras control Canada.

SUSAN: How's my dress look, Daddy?

MICHAEL: Is she the one who eats cigarettes? . . .

MRS. WALL (*finding bits of gum everywhere*): Bobby!!

(*Suddenly the TV emits a bright red glow, and* BOBBY's *slack face assumes an expression of demonic glee. Noises of explosions, car crashes, screams, havoc. Everyone stares at* BOBBY. *TV returns to normal, as does* BOBBY. *Pause. The doorbell rings. Pause.*)

That must be Alvin.

(MRS. WALL *goes to answer the door.* SUSAN *stands up.*)

SUSAN: Are my seams straight, Mommy?

MRS. WALL: You aren't wearing stockings, honey.

(MRS. WALL *opens the door. There stands* ALVIN. *I'm honestly not certain what boys usually wear to high-school proms, but* ALVIN *is dressed appropriately. He holds a corsage.*)

ALVIN: Mrs. Wall? I'm Alvin.

MRS. WALL: Good evening, Alvin. Won't you come in?

ALVIN: Oh, thank you.

(ALVIN *comes in,* MRS. WALL *shuts the door behind him. He seems nervous.* MRS. WALL *looks at him as if he were an enormous Saint Bernard a friend had left in her care for the weekend.*)

MRS. WALL: Well, you've still got some time to kill, kids. I'll go get something to eat.

ALVIN: Oh, well, thank you.

(ALVIN *goes to talk to* SUSAN. *Seeing the corsage in his hand, she sticks out her chest. He awkwardly pins it on. Pause.*)

So. This is the rest of your family, huh?

(SUSAN *giggles.*)

I guess this is the rest of your family, right?

(SUSAN *giggles.*)

Well, I guess I'll talk to your dad, huh?

(SUSAN *giggles.* ALVIN *walks up to* MR. WALL *and stands timidly by, waiting for him to react somehow.*)

Mr. Wall?

(No reaction. ALVIN *sticks his hand out.)*

Mr. Wall?

(No reaction.)

I'm Alvin. Susan's date for the prom?

MR. WALL *(looking up):* Oh! . . . You must be Alvin.

ALVIN: Yes. How do you do?

MR. WALL *(puzzled):* Fine. . . . Have a seat.

(ALVIN sits in an armchair center stage.)

MICHAEL: Pain, baby, pain! . . . Yeah, can you believe it? . . . My own sister and this character. Want to talk to him? . . . No? Okay . . .

ALVIN *(to BOBBY):* So. What's your name?

(Pause.)

MR. WALL: That's Bobby.

ALVIN: Oh, Bobby. *(Pause.)* So how old are you, Bobby?

(Pause.)

MR. WALL: He's twelve. Our littlest.

ALVIN: Twelve. That's nice. *(Pause.)* So. Twelve years old, huh, Bobby? What's this you're watching?

(Pause.)

MR. WALL: It's a cartoon.

ALVIN: Ah. So it is.

(ALVIN follows the cartoon for a while.)

Hm. Y'know, I used to watch cartoons when I was your age, Bobby. I've never seen one quite like this before, though— My God, that cat's carrying a chain saw! *(To* SUSAN, *somewhat alarmed.)* Does he watch a whole lot of this?

(SUSAN *nods, smiling. Suddenly the TV throws another fit, at the end of which* MRS. WALL *enters with a tray on which are a bowl of potato chips, a smaller bowl full of drippy white paste of some kind, a pitcher of red stuff, and a stack of disposable cups.)*

MRS. WALL: Ta-daaaaa!

(MRS. WALL *sets the tray down.* BOBBY *comes miraculously to life.)*

MR. WALL *(throwing aside his paper):* Heyyy, this looks good.

MICHAEL: Yeah, yeah. . . . Look, catch you later, babe. Food's here. . . . Yeah. Strawberry, I think. . . . Mine too. . . . Bye. *(Hangs up.)*

MR. WALL: Ah, honey, you sure know what to bring three hungry men at the end of the day.

BOBBY: Yeah, Mom, this sure is good.

ALVIN: Yes, thank you, Mrs. Wall.

MRS. WALL: No trouble at all, boys.

(MR. WALL *extends his hand to* ALVIN, *palm up.)*

MR. WALL: So, Alvin—gimme five!

(ALVIN *reluctantly slaps Mr. Wall's palm, then offers him his own, which* MR. WALL *slaps with gusto.*)

All rahhht! *(To* MRS. WALL.) Alvin and I were just digging some hand jive, honey.

MICHAEL *(to* ALVIN): Don't worry about Dad. When the keys get liquid, the curves start laughing.

MRS. WALL *(to* ALVIN): Come on, you've got to eat your potato chips if you want to be healthy.

ALVIN: Oh, well, thank you, but I'm not hungry.

MRS. WALL *(waving a potato chip under his nose):* You sure . . . ? *(She begins to sing.)*
They've got that ripple-y, snackety flavor, that makes you say . . .

ALL *(except* ALVIN, *who looks bewildered):*
Hey! Those must be Fantasti-Chips!

ALVIN: I really think Susan and I should get going . . .

SUSAN: Come on, Alvin, it won't matter if we're a *bit* late. Besides, you haven't even touched your Slippity-Dip.

(SUSAN *pushes the bowl toward* ALVIN. *He stares at it in obvious disgust.*)

ALVIN *(weakly):* My *what?*

MICHAEL: You know, *Slippity-Dip. (Begins singing.)*
When you're feeling blue . . .

SUSAN *(picking it up):*
You know what to do . . .

BOBBY:
Just reach for a can of that slippity goo . . .
ALL *(except* ALVIN):
You peel off the lid . . .

(Everyone makes a popping noise in unison.)

And pick up a chip . . .

(Everyone reaches over and picks up a chip, except for ALVIN *and* MRS. WALL, *who puts the potato chip in her hand into Alvin's hand which she then holds up by the wrist.)*

Don't ask questions,
On your mark, get set, dip!

(The family all dip their potato chips, pull them out, and pop them into their mouths in one smooth scooping motion, except for MRS. WALL *who plunges Alvin's unsuspecting hand into the bowl up to the wrist.*

ALVIN: Hey . . .

(Before he can say anything, MRS. WALL *has shoved the potato chip into his open mouth, and he takes it reflexively.* MRS. WALL *holds his dripping hand aloft and waits for him to swallow it, while she solemnly hums along with the rest of the family the tune of the commercial ditty.)*

MR. WALL *(over the humming, in a TV-announcer voice):* Slippity-Dip—the dip that makes you sexy, rich, happy, and intelligent. In strawberry, lemon, grape, or new pork! *(Quietly and hastily.)* Batteries not included.

(With the conclusion of their little song, the family turns its attention to ALVIN, *who looks extremely confused and frightened. Finally he swallows the potato chip. The tension around him vanishes immediately.)*

MRS. WALL: Now you'll be sexy, rich, happy, and intelligent.

*(*ALVIN *is already beginning to seem just a little woozy.)*

SUSAN: You don't look well, Alvin. Have some Sugar-Ade.

*(*SUSAN *pours a cupful of red fluid for him from a pitcher.)*

ALVIN: No, really . . .

MICHAEL: It's *really* good.

ALVIN: No, I'm fine, thank you.

MR. WALL: C'mon, Alvin, it's good for you. There's a full day's supply of vitamin C in every cubic foot. Bobby here's been drinking it all his life.

ALVIN: But isn't that the stuff that . . . causes brain damage?

BOBBY *(staring at* ALVIN *with wide, dreamy eyes)*: Oh, no, it's *wonderful.* It's like . . . *heaven.*

ALVIN: Do you have any milk?

MICHAEL: *Milk!?* Only *quimbies* drink milk!

SUSAN: If you're cool, you drink *Sugar-Ade.*

(Pause. The whole family stares at ALVIN, *who stares at the cup, terrified. He looks up at them.)*

BOBBY *(quietly and seriously):* Drink it or I'll kill you.

*(*ALVIN *believes him. He takes one sip. Pause.)*

ALVIN: Why, it's not bad.

MRS. WALL: We told you.

*(*ALVIN *finishes the drink. Everybody is smiling all of a sudden, passing cups back and forth and drinking Sugar-Ade.)*

ALVIN: Could I have some more of that dip?

ALL *(except* ALVIN): Yes. Of course. Sure. All you want. *(And the like.)*

ALVIN *(between bites):* You know, it's the funniest thing. When I first came here this evening, I thought you people . . . I don't know, I felt really nervous about meeting you. Sort of as if you didn't like me or something.

(Everyone laughs.)

MICHAEL: Oh, you don't have to feel that way, Alvin. You're one of us now.

(Laughter stops. Brief pause.)

MR. WALL: Almost.

ALVIN: What?

VOICE OF TV NEWSCASTER: At the top of tonight's local news headlines, the mutilated body of yet another teenager was found in the suburbs today. The body, which remains unidentified, was seen skateboarding up and down Main Street, listening to a Walkman and singing "We Are the World."

(The family surround Alvin's chair. All watch the news.)

The police are convinced the slayings are actually *human sacrifices* performed by a bizarre ancient cult that has resurfaced in our nation's suburbs. The rite is said to entail the enticement of a victim by an irresistible enchantress (SUSAN *giggles)* and the ingestion of a previous victim's brain and blood, the preparation of which involves mashing the brains into a thin, drippy paste and collecting the blood in ceremonial chalices.

(The family slowly turn their eyes on ALVIN.)

Perhaps the most shocking fact related to these cases is that having had their brains and blood removed, the victims *do not die.* Reports indicate that they actually join the cult and live on in their new environment quite contentedly. We'll be back with more of that, though, after this word.

MR. WALL: Excuse me a moment.

(MR. WALL *exits.*)

VOICE OF FIRST TV ANNOUNCER *(a different speaker, in a rapid-fire voice):* They say the pen is mightier than the sword . . . but try doing *this* with a pen. *(Hideous sound effect of something, like a baby, being chopped apart.)* That's why there's such a thing as the electrodecimator, which can now be yours through this exclusive TV offer at the unbelievably low, low price of five-ninety-nine! The electrodecimator can cut . . . *(Hideous sound effect.)*

(Enter MR. WALL *carrying a device something like an electric carving knife, except maybe with more blades, which he plugs in and turns on. A chain saw might be interesting. Having made sure it's in working order, he shuts off the lights. Only the blue light of the TV remains. He advances toward* ALVIN.*)*

Shred. *(Hideous sound effect.)* Mangle. *(Hideous sound effect.)* And much, much more! Don't forget, order now! Here's how!

(During the following, the family tips Alvin's chair over backward, so his feet are all that can be seen of him, while MR. WALL *positions himself behind him.)*

VOICE OF SECOND TV ANNOUNCER *(speaking fast enough to make the words pretty much indecipherable):* Send check or money order to Electrodecimator, 02820, Mackanacka, Diddlydoo, or save

COD charges by calling 1-800-220-4400. This product can*not* be bought in any store, so order now!

VOICE OF NEWSCASTER: Although the police have numerous extremely accurate and detailed descriptions of the cult members and their whereabouts, they say they'll need a great deal more to limit the suspects to any fewer than twenty million.

(MR. WALL *turns on the device and lowers it on* AL-VIN.)

When asked how the crimes had been distinguished as human sacrifices rather than murders, the chief of police replied that none of the victims evidenced any sign of having resisted.

BLACKOUT

PETER GETTY

I was born in New York in 1965 and raised in San Francisco. For the past five years I've lived on the East Coast, attending prep school and college. I began writing plays in letters to friends when I was in sixth grade, usually as a means by which to express more fully my feelings for a person or thing. I would list as major influences on my writing old Warner Brothers cartoons and commercials.

About the Play

I wrote *A New Approach to Human Sacrifice* in the spring of 1982 for a high-school play-writing class. The ending as it is now, however, was not conceived until December of the same year, between roughly midnight and a last-minute deadline of six in the morning, for a staged reading at the Circle Rep. Since then, I have added a few gags and shortened the occasional monologue, but the play is essentially the same.

I guess it's basically a complaint about our national trend toward the distillation of fun—the methodical extraction, that is to say, from books, movies, plays, music, of everything that is not in and of itself *fun,* presumably on the assumption that something easier to digest is better to eat. Postwar American suburbia, to the best of my ability to judge such things, is a sort of world-within-a-world that has evolved entirely independently of intellect or feeling. *A New Approach to Human Sacrifice* might be considered a guess as to what they have instead. To avoid seeming *entirely* sanctimonious, by the way, I've also tried to make it fun.

MEETING THE WINTER BIKE RIDER

by Juan Nunez
(age seventeen when play was written)

CHARACTERS

MARK, an animated sixteen-year-old boy
TONY, a fourteen-year-old boy

The attendant's room in an old-fashioned gas station.

The set is small and cluttered, weighted with years of oil and grease. Still, it is "gas station–clean." A door leads into the room, downstage right. A desk and swivel chair, upstage right. On the desk is a coffeepot and some books and magazines. There is a stool beside it. Several large windows (suggested) are downstage center. Beyond: gas pumps, sky.

A night in early March.

The present. MARK *is seated at the desk reading a newspaper. He finishes a section of the paper, folds it, and tosses it onto the floor behind him. He thinks better of his action, retrieves the discarded section, and continues reading. He wears soiled blue jeans, a sweatshirt, and a very long scarf.*

TONY *enters from downstage right. He is walking his ten-speed bike, holding the rear wheel above the ground. He seems somehow fragile, and yet he is also graceful. He wears coordinating corduroy pants, shirt, and sweater. His clothes are wet in patches and torn in places.*

TONY *stops before the door, knocks, and* MARK *waves him in.*

TONY *(entering):* I was walking past and I saw the lights on. *(Pause.)* I was hoping you'd still be open.

MARK: I'm afraid we're not. What do you need?

TONY: I could use some pliers. The chain fell off my bike and it's caught in back.

MARK: All right. Sure.

(MARK *finds the pliers in a drawer of the desk and hands them to* TONY.)

TONY: Thank you.

(TONY *steps outside to fix the bike.* MARK *follows.*)

MARK: You look a little messed up. Fall off your bike?

TONY *(pulling at sweater):* Yeah. I was on a road just across the highway when two cars started racing and I had to swerve.

MARK: You're all right?

TONY: I'm fine.

MARK *(Stretching, he checks his watch):* Hey. Did you know it's almost eleven o'clock?

TONY: No.

MARK: Well, I'm not saying it's late or anything, but the cops are ridiculously strict about curfew, and you don't look like you could pass for eighteen, you know?

TONY *(struggling with bike):* Yeah. Neither do you. How do you avoid it?

MARK *(steadying bike):* They know me. *(Pause.)* Your coming here and asking for pliers is no big thing—I mean, kids do it all the time—but not usually until spring, and so I—

TONY: Haven't you ever seen a winter jogger?

MARK: Yes, but joggers dress for the weather and you—

TONY: Listen. My front tire's flat. Do you have an inner tube I could use?

MARK: Only if your front tire's from a car.

TONY: Oh.

(The chain is fixed; TONY *hands* MARK *the pliers.* TONY *stands, not sure what to do next.* MARK *walks around him.)*

MARK: You're not from around here, are you?

TONY: Why do you say that?

MARK: Oh, I don't know. Your clothes, maybe. Anyway, Steger isn't that big, and I don't remember having seen you before.

TONY: Steger? I'm in Steger?

MARK *(amused):* Don't you know?

TONY: I'm just riding. I didn't—I never bothered to check the street signs. *(Reflecting.)* I was never very good with street names.

MARK: I guess not.

TONY: Then . . . I am in Steger, right?

MARK: Sure, you're in Steger. You're nowhere. This town is something like an armpit. *(Slight pause.)* Where should you be?

TONY *(shrugging his shoulders):* In bed.

(Surprised, MARK *gives a delayed laugh.* TONY *smiles, also surprised.)*

In Tinley Park.

MARK *(whistles):* That's a long walk. You want to use the phone and call for a ride?

TONY *(too quickly):* No.

MARK: You're going to walk home, then?

TONY: I guess I'll have to. *(He looks around.)*

MARK: Well . . . I'll be here for a while longer.

You can come in and warm up if you want. I don't mind.

TONY: Yeah. That might be smart.

MARK *(standing in doorway):* It's what I'd do.

(TONY enters, pulls at his sweater and grimaces. He rubs his arms. MARK watches him, then lifts a soiled flannel shirt from a nail on the wall above the desk and tosses it to TONY.)

MARK: Here. You may be a winter bike rider, but you've still got to be cold.

TONY: Thanks.

(TONY hesitates, then puts on the shirt.)

MARK *(sitting down behind desk):* Well, a can of pop? Coffee? Talk, maybe?

TONY *(knowingly):* Trying to make sense out of things? *(He stands by the window.)*

MARK: Well . . . it doesn't look like your bike ride was planned.

TONY: Yeah?

MARK: Sure. Look at you. From where I stand this doesn't look casual at all.

TONY *(sitting):* Really?

MARK: Really. I mean, where could you be going on a bike? A friend's house? The store? Not out in Steger; not this far. You would have gotten a ride, been dropped off . . . unless the car wasn't running.

(TONY *stands, begins pacing.*)

MARK: Was it important that you ride out here?

TONY: Do you have to know?

MARK *(hurt):* No. If you don't want to talk, that's fine with me. I'll just read or something.

TONY: You sound upset.

MARK: Just disappointed. If you were me, wouldn't you want to know what you were doing here?

TONY: I couldn't say.

MARK: If all you really want to do is stand quietly and get warm in this room, say so. All right?

TONY: All right.

(*Silence.*)

MARK *(offhand):* If you're wondering . . . the reason why I'm here after hours is because I like reading all alone. It's relaxing, quiet.

TONY *(agreeing):* Yeah. I like things quiet.

MARK: Was it quiet when you were riding?

TONY *(shaking head):* Boy, you just snuck that one in there. Yes, it was quiet. Gave me time to think.

MARK: But no time to read street signs.

TONY: You want to talk so you can make fun of me?

MARK: Sorry . . . no. (*Slight pause.*) So what brings you to Steger?

TONY: Not a thing.

MARK: Hmmm. . . . You do know you're going

away from, and not heading to, Tinley Park. *(Slight pause.)* What's Tinley Park like?

TONY: Like Steger.

MARK *(sighing):* I was really hoping you'd want to talk.

TONY: Why?

MARK: Why?

TONY: Yes. Why?

MARK *(as if the answer were obvious):* Because this is the perfect setting. I mean, look at us, two perfect strangers dumped at a gas station. We'll probably never see each other again. I like this. Usually the only time this kind of thing happens is when I'm waiting in line somewhere or when I'm in an elevator with a stranger, but then the time is so short, all I can do is act like I'm blind or something. Isn't that stupid? (TONY *shrugs.*) Tell me, while riding in a car at night, did you ever cross your eyes so that the streetlights would blur, and pretend that you were in a movie?

(TONY *begins to answer and* MARK *cuts him off.*)

I knew it! See? I'm a movie.

TONY *(a pained expression):* And the rest of the time you're Clark Kent, right?

MARK: Come on. I'm a movie.

TONY: Okay.

MARK: I am!

TONY: Okay!

MARK: Wait. Maybe I should say I'm making a

movie. Yes, that's better. I act, write, direct. If I don't like an actor, I just cut him out. If I don't like a scene, I change it. My movie runs all the time, and right now you're in it and everything is really right for talking, or at least it could be if you let it.

TONY: You always this free with strangers?

MARK: Only when I don't know who they are. *(Slight pause.)* You think I'm silly, don't you.

TONY: No.

MARK: Yes, you do . . . for a sixteen-year-old anyway, right?

TONY: I always wanted to be in a movie.

MARK: I'll bet you're a good actor. . . . And since I forgot to do this earlier *(He holds out his hand.),* my name's Mark.

TONY: Tony.

(They shake hands.)

MARK: People say I'm pushy. I don't mean to be a pain.

TONY: You're not pushy, but—

MARK: But I'm a pain, right?

TONY: No. You're . . . friendly.

MARK: But friendless.

TONY: So, you're somebody making a movie. Can't you just change the script?

MARK: No, I'd . . . like some real actors to play the parts. They really aren't that hard to play. *(He looks at* TONY.*)*

TONY: Tinley Park is like anywhere. The kids play

baseball, Pac-Man; they mow lawns, work at Mc-Donald's, save up and buy a car and then drive it in and out of the driveway.

MARK: Really? *(Excited but restraining himself.)* What would your mother say if she walked in here now?

TONY: My mother? I guess she'd ask me what I did to my clothes, and tell me that I'm gonna get sick, and to take off this filthy shirt of yours.

MARK *(aside):* Terrific. *(Then.)* How about your father?

TONY: I don't know.

MARK: Any sisters?

(TONY *shakes his head no.)*

Brothers?

(TONY *shakes his head again.)*

TONY: Wait. I did have a brother, but . . . he's dead . . . before I was born.

MARK *(with pleased emphasis):* A Freudian omission!

TONY: Excuse me?

MARK: Oh. That means you made yourself forget that you had a brother. Why?

TONY: You are a little pushy.

MARK *(offended):* And you're a little lost.

TONY *(walking to door):* I didn't start this conversation.

MARK *(standing):* All right, all right, all right. I'm sorry. Okay?

(TONY stops.)

I don't—I don't want to see you leave now.
TONY: Why not?
MARK: My movie. . . . *(He sits.)* Are you leaving? *(Pause.)* It's cold.
TONY *(relaxing):* Yeah. I'll stay.
MARK: Good.

(There is a silence. MARK *picks at the small balls of lint on his socks.)*

TONY: Don't you want to talk anymore?
MARK *(offhand):* I don't know.
TONY: Are you mad at me?

(MARK shakes his head no.)

Then ask me something.
MARK: Are you having fun?
TONY: I don't think so. *(He sits.)*
MARK: Oh. Well, what do you do for fun?
TONY: Fun? *(Thinking.)* Next door to my house—two houses over, actually—there's a parking lot which is always filled with cars. And there's something unnerving about walking through a parking lot filled with cars at night . . . which is what I do, get unnerved at night by walking through a parking lot filled with cars.
MARK: And that's fun?

TONY: No, but it kills time. At least it used to kill time. I guess I'll find something else to take its place.

MARK: What was fun about it?

TONY (smiles, remembering): This is embarrassing. (Pause.) Pickup trucks are scary, but only from the back. Vans are all right because you can scare the hell out of yourself if you keep thinking someone's gonna jump out and run at you. Cars don't do much for me, but . . . there was this station wagon. I was looking through its back window, and all of a sudden this dog that was inside jumped up and started barking right in my face. It was incredibly frightening. You should have seen me run. I'm glad no one was around.

MARK: Why?

TONY: It sounds like something a little kid would do.

MARK: So what? You're not exactly old.

TONY: No.

MARK (walking around desk to sit opposite TONY): But you do seem older; you're very controlled. Do you have a lot of girlfriends?

TONY: Oh, no. I mean, I would like one . . . but, no, I don't. My . . . image isn't all that great. (Slight pause.) What's the big rush to have a girlfriend, anyway? I'm not old enough to have a job, so I have no money to spend. I don't have a car or even know someone who has a car, so I can't take a girl anywhere.

MARK: You could go out with older girls.

TONY: Hah. That'd be wild. My parents would love that, some woman driving up in a Firebird to take me to a movie. Besides, she'd probably be real aggressive. She'd probably want to hold hands or make out all the time in front of people or something.

MARK: You wouldn't like that.

TONY: Well, I don't know. I guess it's not so much that— I mean, yes . . . it is that . . . being public. I can't stand it when people make out and stuff in a movie or at school. *(Trailing off.)* Gross, all that touching.

MARK: All what?

TONY: All . . . touching. It's demanding, you know. Girls demand it. I think I don't mind it, but it's not for me, not all the time.

(Pause.)

MARK: Anything else?

TONY: Like what?

MARK: Like, sometimes I feel isolated, so different that I almost think I'm abnormal. I don't think I am, but when I look hard at people, I think that they're orbiting around me, and when I look harder, I can see them rip the air.

TONY *(interested):* Do you have many girlfriends?

MARK: No. I had one; just broke up with my first a few weeks ago. She was a real letdown. *(Slight pause.)* I'll agree with you, in a way, about the demands and hardships of having a girlfriend. Let me tell you, Tony, most girls don't want someone they can talk to; they want a gerbil, something to pet and water and mother. And I'm not saying this because of one experience; I say it because I've looked around and talked to people. When I broke up with my girlfriend, I told her I was doing it because she was boring, and she was. I told her she wasn't giving me anything. She cried and apologized and it was a touchy scene, but we'd still be friends, right? Now whenever we run into each other I whisk myself away to some nether plane and temporarily cease to exist.

TONY: Why did you go out with her?

MARK: I've intellectualized it, and I decided that we went out because I wanted something memorable. And she was pretty too.

TONY: Don't you think she wanted something memorable?

MARK: I suppose.

TONY (probing): You think you're the most interesting person in the world, don't you. That you should be famous and you're easygoing and one hell of a nice guy, right?

MARK (tight): You're sure talking a lot now.

(TONY *shrugs, self-conscious.* MARK *slides down in his seat and his foot touches Tony's.* TONY *moves.* MARK *touches him again;* TONY *moves.* MARK* *touches Tony's foot a third time, and as* TONY *moves,* MARK *kicks his foot aside.)*

MARK: It bothers you that my foot touched yours.

TONY: I don't know.

MARK *(irritated):* You do, because it does, and I think it's ridiculous. I remember going to the show with a friend of mine whom I've known for years, and he wanted to sit with a seat between us because he said it looks better. What is that? I'm not going with him so I can yell to him from across the theater. Little kids don't worry about those things. And I've known this guy practically all my life, we slept over each other's houses and hung around and all that; but then I touch a foot and, Oh, my God! Move your foot!

TONY: What can you do. People are like that.

MARK: I suppose they are. *(He tucks his feet behind his stool.)* Well, at least we're talking.

(Silence, then TONY *is startled by a sudden gust of wind.)*

TONY: Listen to that wind. Sounds like it's going to blow the building down.

MARK: Isn't that true. But I doubt it. I've been told that these windows have been up for thirty years.

TONY: Really? *(He walks to the windows.)* That's hard to believe. Just think, these windows have been around longer than I have.

MARK (*stands beside* TONY): Yeah. You warmer yet?

TONY: Why? Are you getting ready to leave?

MARK: No . . . not yet.

TONY: Good.

(*Pause.*)

I like your selection of gas. (*He points.*) Regular and regular.

MARK: So we're not exactly contemporary.

TONY: That's good, though. It gives the place style. (*Distant.*) If this window were in my room, it would look great. Of course, I couldn't look out of it—my room's downstairs—but this way it would never get broken. (*Pause.*) You know, I always wonder what the parents of killers and murderers think, or what they thought about when their kids were growing up. You think they knew?

MARK: I don't know. Maybe.

TONY: I wonder what my parents think I'll be?

MARK: I hope not a killer.

TONY: I like to draw, and I'm not that bad, but my parents don't think of art as a possible career. There's no money in it.

MARK: You want to be an artist?

TONY: Yeah. Why not.

MARK: Well, it seems to me—

TONY (*loudly*): Are you going to tell me to do whatever I feel and who cares what they think?

(MARK *is silent.*)

Sorry.

(TONY *walks around room.*)

You know, no one knows I'm here? They know I'm gone, but they don't know where. I wonder what they're doing now?

MARK *(sitting behind desk):* Probably calling the police and all the hospitals.

TONY: More likely they're calling friends and relatives. Or they might be checking the stores.

MARK: Have you done this before?

TONY: A couple of times, when I get upset or something. I know it's childish, but what else am I supposed to do? Hop in a car I don't know how to drive, and go somewhere? Move away? The options aren't great. Still, tonight wasn't so bad.

MARK: No. *(Pause.)* Tony? Do me a favor and tell me why you're here.

TONY: I— Well, it centers around my getting in a fight, I guess. It was stupid because I hate fights. I always run from them. I don't think I'm afraid, but I always run. Except today. Today I got in a fight, and I've never been in a fight before.

MARK: And you lost.

TONY: No.

MARK: You won?

(TONY *nods.*)

Then what's the problem?

TONY: The problem is that I didn't want to fight him.

MARK: And that bothers you? I mean, I guess it should . . . but if this guy was pushing you around, well, what else could you do?

TONY: Probably nothing.

MARK: All right, then. Just relax. Don't let it bother you. You did what you should have, what you had to do, anyway, and it's over.

TONY: Yeah. *(Nods.)* But I started it.

MARK: What? Why?

TONY: Oh, how should I know?

MARK: What do you mean "how should I know"? You hit him.

TONY: I hit him but I'm not sure why. *(He begins to explain, then stops himself.)* Forget it.

MARK *(excited):* No! This is cruel. This is interesting as hell. Don't do this. People always do this to me.

TONY *(He looks at MARK, turns away):* I'm one of those kids that everyone picks on.

MARK *(struggling to make the connection):* Yeah.

TONY: My parents know this. Once they saw me getting teased and pushed around in front of our house by some kids. It didn't bother my mother so much as it bothered my father. He wanted me to do something, defend myself, I guess. He wanted to see what I'd do, which was nothing, and then he acted like it never happened. But I knew he was watching.

MARK *(still struggling):* Yeah.

TONY: So I let him down!

(Pause.)

TONY: My brother wasn't average . . . he got a lot of trophies from baseball and ribbons and things from school. There are pictures . . . in my parents' bedroom . . . of him and my father together, and I can see that my father was real proud of him. He still is, you know?

MARK: Yeah. That's—that's weird.

TONY: My father used to spend a lot of time with me when I was younger, trying to get me into sports or something, but I wasn't any good. Now he never bothers with me. I don't think he expects anything from me.

MARK: Have you told him how you feel?

TONY: Yeah.

MARK: And?

TONY: I still feel the same way.

MARK: So tell him again.

TONY: Oh, it won't do any good.

MARK: How do you know?

TONY *(explosive):* Because I do! *(Slight pause.)* To-day after school this fat kid bumped into me and I dropped all of my books and I got upset. I was pretty upset already, so I really bore down on this kid, teasing him about his weight and his mother. And he was really getting hurt but he wouldn't do anything. Then everybody started telling me to beat him up, but I didn't want to, so I kept cutting him down. Then they were saying that I was scared. So I hit him. But I wasn't really mad anymore. And he just stood there and took it, which really pissed me off. Do you follow me? *(Slight pause.)* I went home. My parents ask what happened, and my father is very proud of me. Good. Great. What I hate most and he's proud. Wouldn't that— *(He catches himself.)* Wouldn't that bother you?

MARK *(empathic):* Yeah. I think it would.

TONY *(protracted sigh):* Yeah. So I just left. I was so disgusted, I just left. I don't know. God I— *(Laughs.)* I feel so old.

(Silence.)

MARK: So what are you gonna do now?

TONY *(standing):* Now? Now I guess I'll probably go home.

MARK: Well . . . yeah. That's about the smartest thing to do.

TONY *(loud):* I know, I know. I always do that. Sometimes I wish I'd quit trying to make sense out of things . . . sense!

(On the word "sense" TONY sits down heavily on the stool, tipping it back. He falls.)

MARK *(amused):* Are you all right?

TONY *(shaking head):* Yeah, yeah. How come you aren't laughing?

MARK *(laughs):* I don't know. I guess I didn't think to.

TONY *(A moment, then he laughs):* God, but you're weird.

MARK: What?

TONY: Don't worry. *(Considering himself.)* I'm a jerk who falls off chairs.

MARK: So what? You fell off and big deal.

TONY: Yes, big deal. I've just ruined your movie. I'm not much of an actor, am I?

MARK: No, no. You worked out good. You even un-bored me.

TONY *(standing):* Yeah, but I bet you'd have liked it better if I had never shown up tonight, huh? Am I right?

MARK: Geez, Tony. Listen to me. I'm telling you—

TONY *(Suddenly playful. With near hysteria; hysterical energy):* Tell me the truth. I can take it. *(He stands in front of MARK.)* Do I get in your hair? *(He runs his hands through Mark's hair. A second, then MARK reacts to the pun.)* Do I irritate you? (TONY grabs Mark's ears.) Sorry. But I need you. *(He knees MARK.)* And you're not going anywhere. I got my eye on you. *(He puts his eye to Mark's shoulder. MARK grabs TONY by the arms.)*

MARK *(firm; unsure):* That's—that's funny. *(He*

runs his hand through Tony's hair.) You're funny,
you know that? You're all right. You're all right.

(A moment, then TONY *impulsively tries to embrace*
MARK. MARK *starts and pulls back.)*

TONY: Hey, what's the matter?

*(*MARK *is motionless.)*

Hey, I didn't mean anything.
MARK: Okay. Calm down. I believe you.
TONY: Oh, brother.
MARK: Wait. I know what was—
TONY: Forget it, Mark. Okay? Hey—hey, listen.
I've got to go. It's late. *(He awkwardly shakes
Mark's hand.)* I'm glad we met.

*(*TONY *walks to the door.)*

MARK: Tony, wait. Don't leave now and make me
feel stupid.
TONY: Forget it, okay?
MARK *(A moment, then he speaks):* Sure.

*(*TONY *steps outside. He starts to walk quickly away,
pushing his bike.)*

TONY *(stopping momentarily):* I hope your movie
went well. It's as good as most.
MARK *(from doorway):* You're wearing my shirt.

*(*TONY *touches the shirt.)*

Keep it, you know?

(TONY *nods and continues walking, exiting stage right.* MARK *closes the door and, for a moment, stands in the middle of the room. He picks up the fallen stool. The lights fade.*)

CURTAIN

JUAN NUNEZ

I began writing when I was fifteen, the year I dropped out of my local high school. During that time I wrote stories, some first poems, and my only play to date, *Meeting the Winter Bike Rider.* I sent the resulting portfolio to the Interlochen Arts Academy in Interlochen, Michigan, and was accepted into their creative writing program, from which I graduated in 1984. I plan to attend New York University. I am currently living and working in Steger, Illinois.

About the Play

Though the play is fictitious, *Bike Rider* has its origins in a real, old-fashioned gas station in Steger, Illinois. I walked my town almost every night the winter of 1981, and I always found myself standing across the street from, and staring at, the gas station. It did seem the perfect setting for a conversation, and as is the case with many writers (or so they say), the play was "waiting" there for me. Once discovered, it seemingly created itself, blooming full before me: the moth of my mind then drew me to its large windows, the attendant in the room, bent, like filament in a bulb, framed in a yellow rectangle of light.

So much for rejuvenating the light-bulb-idea cliché.

Dreams and inspiration aside, writing is hard work. It is a physical act that starts in the hands (snapping fingers, drumming desks), moves to the head (which is repeatedly scratched), to the back and eyes (which are sore from rereading each line ten times), and finally returns to the hands when they attempt to rub these aches from the body. The greatest misconception beginning writers have is that writing takes place in the mind. It does not. It is hard manual labor.

Performing is also hard labor, and I have nothing but respect for the undying energy and agile creativity of the director of *Bike Rider* and the actors. This idea of work, of integrating sense and physical things, was nothing new to them (and shouldn't be for a writer, either—playwright or poet): it is the very essence of theater. During rehearsals I heard the director use two words more than any others: *organic,* that which makes the scene a believable, living moment; and *flesh,* as in to flesh out a line, an emotion, a character who is real. To see the transition from page to stage was a first for me, a unique opportunity. The Festival taught me well. Dreams are of the body. Writing shows us what is possible.

SCRAPS
A Play in Six Scenes

by Tagore J. McIntyre
(age ten when play was written)

CHARACTERS

Pete, a well-liked Anglo boy
Mary, an Indian girl; Pete's friend
Dillon, an Indian boy; Pete's friend
Tim, a quiet, thoughtful Indian boy
Benny Yellowfeather, an Indian boy with problems
Mr. Conway, the playground duty teacher
John, a disliked Indian boy
Jimmy, a slightly retarded Indian boy; John's
brother
Marlinda, a tough Indian girl
Mr. Tillinig, an insensitive schoolteacher
Other students may be in background
SCRAPS requires a cast of ten (six boys, two
girls, two men) with extras as desired.

Scene One

The playground of a school on the edge of an Indian reservation.

It is morning. PETE, MARY, *and* DILLON *are playing basketball.* TIM *sits on the bleachers.* BENNY *sits nearby watching.* DILLON *makes a basket.*

PETE: Hey, Tim! Want to play basketball?

TIM: No, thanks! I'm drawing a picture.

PETE: Okay! Hey, my ball.

JOHN *(approaches the group):* Hey, you guys! I'll give you this Coke if you let me play.

MARY: Go away, Boney.

DILLON: Yeah, get outta here, Boney!

PETE *(secretively):* Wait, Mary, come here.

MARY: What?

PETE *(secretively):* Mary, my watch says that there's only ten minutes until the bell rings. Get the Coke from John and he won't play very long anyway!

MARY *(back with group):* All right, John, you can play for the Coke. *(Takes Coke from* JOHN.)

CONWAY *(walks up holding a book which he has been reading while standing).* Boys, there is a teachers workshop still going on in the cafeteria. You'll still get to play for, maybe, another half hour, and I'll still be your duty teacher.

PETE *(glances at* MARY): Okay, thanks, Mr. Conway.

(MR. CONWAY *walks away reading his book.*)

JOHN: Well, let's play!

PETE: Oh, I don't want to.

(Group breaks up.)

JOHN *(looks confused, then angry; yells at his bigger brother who has been standing by himself):* Jimmy, Jimmy, come 'ere. Beat this guy up for me. He won't let me play. I gave him my Coke.

JIMMY *(strolls over, hands in his pockets, grinning):* Why aren't you dummies lettin' my brother play?

DILLON: Hey, John, why do you always have to call your big retarded brother?

PETE *(to JIMMY):* For one thing, we're not dummies, and for another, this guy's a pest. Just like your stupid friend Benny Yellowfeather.

JIMMY: Yellowfeather's not my friend, joker. Give back the Coke John gave you.

PETE: Sure, why not? Who wants a Coke from a wino's kid? *(Throws Coke toward JOHN. It falls and squirts on the ground.)*

JIMMY *(faces PETE, ready to fight):* Stupid! I'm gonna beat you up!

PETE *(laughs):* Come on, man, I don't want to—

JIMMY: Chicken!

DILLON: He's not a chicken. He doesn't look like you.

JIMMY: Shut up!

DILLON: You shut up!

JIMMY: Make me!

DILLON: Give me some wood and nails. I'll make you so this reservation will have two blockheads! *(Looks at others for laughter.)*

JIMMY *(turns to fight DILLON)*: I'll show you, Big Mouth!

DILLON: I wouldn't try anything, Wino. Here, I got something for you. *(Punches Jimmy in the stomach.)* It's called a Navajo punch!

(JIMMY starts to cry.)

Want me to do it some more, Retard?

(JIMMY runs offstage. JOHN runs after him, his head down.)

BENNY *(approaches from the bleachers)*: Can I play with the ball?

MARY: Benny Yellowfeather, get out of here!

PETE: Come on, Benny, and let you kick it out in the trees? No way!

BENNY *(whining)*: I won't.

PETE: Listen. This ball belongs to Mr. Tillinig, right?

BENNY *(looking bored)*: Uh-huh.

PETE: And I'm the one who took it from the class to play with, right?

BENNY: Yeah.

PETE: If you lose it, who's gonna pay for it? You already have a record of losing balls!

BENNY *(getting mad)*: I won't lose it!

PETE: Okay. *(Bounces the ball to BENNY.)* But you

know what will happen if I end up paying for Mr. Tillinig's basketball! Come on, Mary, Dillon. Let's go somewhere else.

(All three walk downstage and BENNY *tries to shoot baskets upstage.* MARY *and* DILLON *look at* PETE *questioningly.)*

PETE: Well, if we play, John will want to play.

MARLINDA *(rushes up to* DILLON, *her hands on her hips; looks mean):* Hey, Dillon, I heard that you said something bad about me!

*(*MARY *and* PETE *step back.)*

DILLON: Hey, I didn't say any— *(*MARLINDA *socks him in the mouth.)*

MARLINDA: Jimmy told me! He don't lie! Now listen up. I just want you to remember that I don't want to hear nothin' from you. *(Stomps off.)*

DILLON *(rubbing his mouth):* I don't either!

PETE: Where's my ball, Benny?!

BENNY *(ignores what* PETE *said):* Hey, Rich Boy, you're getting fat, you know that? You might rip those new pants you got on!

DILLON: Who's getting fat?

BENNY: Ole Pete.

DILLON: Well, compared to you, he's—

PETE: Cool it, Dillon. I'll settle this. Benny, you want your face turned inside out? At least I don't have a washrag on like you do!

BENNY: Just kidding, P-Pete.

PETE: Now, where's the ball?

DILLON *(grinning, looks at the others):* I suppose it went out to lunch!

BENNY: Oh, I forgot. I left it out by the bastketball goal.

DILLON *(points over to the goal):* Really? I don't see any ball! *(Runs over to the goal, searches area, comes back.)* No ball!

PETE: Now you've done it this time, Yellowfeather! You've lost another ball, and this time it's on me!

BENNY *(shrugs):* You can't prove it to Tillinig! Ha! Ha! Ha!

(Benny tries to run off, but DILLON grabs him. TIM closes his drawing pad, gets up, walks toward the others.)

MARY *(to BENNY):* We'll get you for this!

DILLON: We're gonna beat you up if you don't tell Tillinig you're the one who lost the ball. And you have to pay for it!

BENNY: Not me! You checked it out.

PETE *(shoves him):* Look, creep. You're the one in trouble whether you like it or not. Right, Dillon?

(Bell rings. MARY and DILLON nod in agreement as they hurry to the classroom.)

Scene Two

A dreary classroom.

TILLINIG *(wringing hands, biting lips, but trying to smile):* Are all the balls in the ball box?

BENNY: No! Pete lost the basketball.

TILLINIG *(surprised):* Peter, did you lose the basketball?

PETE: No, Mr. Tillinig. Benny did!

TILLINIG: Now. Wait just a minute. Who lost the ball, Ben?

BENNY: Pete. He took it out.

TILLINIG: Who lost the ball, Peter?

PETE *(rolling his eyes):* Benny.

TILLINIG: Come here, boys. You will both get swats.

DILLON: Wait, Mr. Tillinig! It's Benny's fault! I saw the whole thing!

TILLINIG: Now, Dillon, tell us what happened.

DILLON: Well, you see, Benny wanted to play with the basketball that Pete took outside. So Pete let him. Then Benny lost the ball.

TILLINIG: Oh, I see. Ben, come here. Now you're going to tell the class the truth, right?

(BENNY *shrugs.*)

Did you do what Dillon said?

BENNY: No.

TILLINIG: Okay. Are there any other witnesses besides Dillon?

MARY: I saw it too. Benny is lying!

TILLINIG: Okay, Ben. Did you do it?

BENNY *(lowers his head and smiles):* Yes.

TILLINIG: Whoa! Now, you just said that you didn't do it. Now, did you do it or not?

BENNY: Yeah, I did it!

TILLINIG: Okay, come here, Peter.

(PETE *walks up.*)

Now, Ben, say you're sorry!

BENNY *(mutters):* Sorry.

(Class smirks and giggles.)

TILLINIG *(looks at* BENNY): Well, let's see. That'll be sixteen dollars and ninety-eight cents for the basketball.

PETE *(walks back to his desk, next to Dillon's):* Thanks for the backup. That was a close one!

DILLON: Look at Benny. Wonder what he's gonna say now!

BENNY *(waving his arm):* Mr. Tillinig, you know what Pete did? He smashed John's Coke all over the ground!

TILLINIG: John should know better than to bring a Coke to school.

BENNY: But—but—

TILLINIG: No buts! Peter is not in trouble. Now, we're going to have art. Tim, get the drawings that we drew last week out of the cabinet.

TIM: Okay.

TILLINIG: Okay, here is some tape. Put your pictures on the wall.

(Everyone does. Tim's picture looks like this: Sun is shining behind some mountains; silhouette of two boys fighting. TILLINIG *points at Benny's picture.)*

Who's that? Fat Albert?

BENNY *(angrily):* No!

TILLINIG: Well, I don't know! I'm not supposed to, am I?

TIM: I like the colors in your picture a lot, Benny.

BENNY *(turns around, startled):* You do?

TIM: What's that in her hand?

BENNY: It's a board.

TIM: What is she going to do with the board?

BENNY *(makes a face):* What does anybody do with a board? *(Walks away.)*

TILLINIG: Okay, put the art stuff away.

(Everyone does.)

Okay, take out your math books, please.

(JOHN *takes out a little car and starts to play with it; the others take out their math book.*)

TILLINIG *(staring at* JOHN): Take out your math books, please!

(JOHN *doesn't hear him and keeps on playing.* TILLINIG *grabs the car and throws it away.*)

You act as if you're still in kindergarten!

JOHN: Hey, that was my brother Ralph's car! He'll beat me up if he thinks I lost it!

DILLON: Well, then, you can tell your brother that you owe him a new car, Monkey!

(Class laughs; DILLON *looks around, happy.* JOHN *starts to cry.)*

I said Monkey, not Crybaby!

(Class laughs again.)

TILLINIG: Enough is enough. *(Frowning.)* Okay, John, get out your math book. Page two forty-six. Benny! Paper costs a lot of money. Stop wasting it. That's three pages you've wadded up.

(JOHN *passes a note to* TIM. PETE *sees it and grabs it.)*

PETE: Mr. Tillinig. John just passed this note.

TILLINIG: Let's see. *(Opens it; reads it silently.)* Ben, come here and read this to the class.

BENNY *(scared):* "Tim, I hate Mr. Tillinig. Do you? Yes. No."

(Class is silent; some mouths drop open.)

TILLINIG *(sarcastically to* BENNY): Well, this is a fine work of art, John! Tim, what is your answer?

TIM *(speaks calmly):* You know the answer is no. I would have told you myself if I had got the note.

TILLINIG: Okay, for writing the note, John, you don't have to work anymore.

*(*JOHN *looks at* TILLINIG *in awe.)*

Instead, you can go to the principal's office with a note that says for you to get three swats and for you to sit in the office. *(Writes the note.)* Well, you'd better be on your way.

*(*JOHN *leaves the room.)*

Class, do your math.

Scene Three

Classroom, after math.

TILLINIG: Close your math books. You may have free time now.

PETE: Hey, Tim, let's play checkers.
TIM: All right.

(BENNY *hears that* PETE *wants the checkers, and runs to the shelf and gets the game.*)

PETE *(grits his teeth):* Tim and I want to play checkers! Could we play with them?
BENNY: Shut up! I got the checkers first!
TIM: Well, Pete, do you want to draw?
PETE *(glares at* BENNY): Yeah, I guess so.

(TIM *gets paper and hands some to* PETE.)

TIM: Here's some paper.
PETE: Thanks.

(There is a knock on the door. TILLINIG *answers it.)*

CONWAY: It's time for Jimmy to come to special ed.
TILLINIG *(chuckles mockingly):* Jimmy. It's time for special ed!

(Most of the class laughs. JIMMY *gets up, his head down, and walks out the door.)*

TIM: I'm going to draw Batman fighting the Penguin.

(Everyone else is doing something, but BENNY *is standing up holding the checkerboard.* TILLINIG *is grading the math papers.)*

MARLINDA *(to* BENNY): Hey, clown, who do you think you are—the big checker sheriff of the class?

TILLINIG *(holds up a paper):* Well, Ben, you've done it again.

BENNY: What?

TILLINIG: You should know. You've done it a hundred times. How did you ever get in this grade anyway?

DILLON *(to* MARY): Yeah, I wonder how he got in here myself.

MARY: Me too.

TIM *(shows* PETE *his picture):* Finished.

PETE: That's a great picture!

BENNY *(walks over):* That's a dumb picture!

(Bell rings.)

TILLINIG *(looks happy):* Time for recess!

(All go outside except TILLINIG.)

Scene Four

Playground.
   Kids are playing.
PETE *(walking):* Tim, that was really stupid of Benny to say that. He's dumb!

TIM: Yeah, maybe. But I think he was just mad about what happened today. He's usually—

PETE: Why do people act dumb like that?

TIM: When I act dumb, it's usually after my mom and dad had a fight.

PETE: You're not dumb. Haven't you noticed the way he acts? First he lies. Then he tells the truth. I guess you're going to say his parents do the same thing.

TIM: I wasn't going to say that. I don't know why anybody does anything.

(JOHN *comes out of the principal's office.* BENNY *goes up to him.*)

BENNY: How many swats did you get?

JOHN: Shut up! You don't have to tell the whole playground, do you?

BENNY: Hey, I didn't— Oh, go flush your head down the toilet! (*Starts to walk away.*)

JOHN: If I did that, my head would look like yours! (*Hurries after* BENNY.) Who do you think you are, the president? I saw your dad hanging around the bar last night.

BENNY: What were you doing there, waiting for your mom?

JOHN (*yelling*): Well, you look like a monkey! If a monkey came to your house, your mom would think it was you. If you even have a mom!

TIM (*looks really upset*): I'm going back to the room, Pete. See you later.

BENNY *(in John's face):* SHUT UP! Your mom is so fat she looks like Porky Pig! She's always stuffing her mouth! No wonder you're just a bag of bones! Your mother eats all your food!

(JOHN and BENNY start fighting; a crowd gathers around them.)

Scene Five

Classroom.
　　PETE *and* TILLINIG *are seated at their desks.*
TILLINIG: Why don't you want to play outside?
TIM *(drawing):* 'Cause there's a fight.
PETE *(rushes in):* They got some more guys in the fight!
TILLINIG: I'd better check this out. You guys have so many problems. *(Looks annoyed.)* Where is the duty teacher? Probably out reading a book!
PETE *(looks undecided about staying or going, then walks over to* TIM): What are you drawing?
TIM: Just garbage.
PETE: Garbage? Looks like people fighting.
TIM: Well, that is garbage! Don't you see how much garbage is in people's lives? No, you wouldn't. You're just— Sometimes I feel like punching some-

one. But I won't. My people weren't like that. But they changed when you treated them like scraps!

PETE: Hey, why are you getting so mad? I didn't do nothing.

TIM: You SAY you didn't.

PETE: Well, I'm going to go see how the fight's going. *(Leaves the room.)*

(BENNY marches into the room alone; starts writing all over the blackboard, nasty things, a picture showing a noose around someone's neck.)

TIM *(softly):* You really hurt bad, don't you.

BENNY *(turns around as if he were going to fight TIM, but he starts crying and shouts):* I hate everybody! My mom and dad got divorced. My mom hits me every time I go home! She yells at me. Everybody here is— I do everything wrong— *(Breaks down.)* Nobody cares!

TILLINIG *(enters the room; looks angry):* Benny Yellowfeather! Get out here! You are going with me to the principal's office. Right now!

(BENNY gets up, squints, and stares at TILLINIG; he saunters to the door and then rushes out. TIM stares at the chalkboard and what BENNY wrote and drew; his mouth drops open and then he rushes out the door. He does not see JOHN approaching. JOHN stares at TIM who is chasing BENNY. TILLINIG stands looking confused; he stares at chalkboard, appears to be thinking about it.)

Scene Six

Outdoors.
   TIM *chases* BENNY.
TIM: Wait!

(BENNY *doesn't stop, so* TIM *runs up and grabs him. They both fall to the ground and wrestle.*)

BENNY: Go away! You're just like everybody else! No one's my friend!
TIM: Benny, I'm your friend!
TILLINIG (*runs up and, grabbing their shirts, pulls them apart*): I'm sick of you young punks fighting all the time! I don't know what your problem is, but you're going to the principal's office right now!
TIM: Mr. Tillinig, you don't understand—
TILLINIG: I understand more than you do! I've been here thirty years! I was here when the parking lot was a playground, and I saw the gymnasium being built too. You can't tell me what's going on!

(*They walk to the principal's office at the side of the stage; they go inside.*)

JOHN (*rushes up to* PETE): Pete, you know what? Tim and Benny just got sent to the principal's office by Mr. Tillinig! He said they were going to get swats! Hey, Jimmy, Tim and Benny are in the principal's office to get swats!

(Kids crowd around office, waiting. TIM *and* BENNY *walk out.)*

BENNY *(softly to* TIM*):* Y-you shouldn't have got a swat. You didn't deserve it.

*(*TIM *smiles at* BENNY *and lowers his head.* BENNY *looks around and kicks a stone.)*

Thanks.

*(*TIM *and* BENNY *slowly walk away.)*

END

TAGORE J. McINTYRE

I was born in Safford, Arizona, on July 4, 1972. I went to a few schools in Arizona and was taught at home for a year. Right now I live in Sanders. I like to play basketball and listen to music and play the guitar. I hope to buy an electric guitar this summer. When we first came here, my dad was a deputy sheriff. Now both of my parents are junior-high teachers. I will be a sophomore in high school next year.

About the Play

A few years back I saw a poster advertising the Young Playwrights Festival. I decided to try it, and the thing I knew most about was my class. So I wrote *Scraps* and was fortunate enough to win as runner-up. In New York Gerald Chapman and Danny Irvine each directed my play. By watching them, I learned a few things about directing. Just recently I directed a play that I wrote, and it was put on at my school. As for future plans with the Festival, I have a feeling I will write something sometime. I don't know. I'll just have to wait and see.

FIXED UP
A Play in Two Acts

by Patricia Durkin
(age sixteen when play was written)

CHARACTERS

Laura, a teenager
Jeffrey, her escort

ACT ONE

The prom.

LAURA *and* JEFFREY, *two adolescents of reasonably good looks, enter together. She is wearing a typical pastel-colored prom dress; he a black tuxedo. As they arrive at the formally laid table for two, he pulls out her chair. No other tables are evident to the audience.*

LAURA *(tucking her skirt under the chair):* Thank you.

JEFFREY *(seating himself):* Uh—no problem.

LAURA *(slight pause):* They picked a nice place for the prom, didn't they?

JEFFREY: Yes, yes. I like the, uh, walls. The walls are a nice color of . . .

LAURA: Gray.

JEFFREY: Right. *(Slight pause.)* They're—distinctive.

LAURA: I heard the band was good too. *(Craning her neck.)* It's hard to tell from here.

JEFFREY: They did give us one of the more—private—tables.

(Silence.)

JEFFREY: Uh—you look very nice tonight.

LAURA: Thank you.

JEFFREY: That's a nice dress. I like it.

LAURA: Do you *really?*

JEFFREY: Sure . . .

LAURA: My mother picked it out. I wasn't allowed to have my first choice.

JEFFREY: You weren't?

LAURA: No, and I loved it too. It was black, floor-length; this terrific satin . . . no straps and a slit. You should've seen it.

JEFFREY *(with feeling):* Yeah . . . but that's a nice dress too.

(Silence.)

LAURA: I hear you're going to the Massachusetts Institute of Technology.

JEFFREY: Yeah. They, uh, call it MIT . . . for short.

LAURA: Oh, I *know.* That's so great.

JEFFREY: Thanks.

LAURA: Where else?

JEFFREY: Excuse me?

LAURA: Where else did you apply? I mean, you must've tried someplace besides MIT, unless your uncle owns it or something.

JEFFREY *(uncomfortably):* Oh . . . Yale, Harvard, Tufts, Notre Dame, and Brown.

LAURA: What a laundry list!

JEFFREY: Do you know where you'd like to go?

LAURA: Anyplace that'll take me.

JEFFREY: That narrows it right down.

LAURA: Oh, it *does.* I'm not very academic.

JEFFREY: Well, what's your lowest grade?

LAURA: A-minus.

JEFFREY: Oh, you should be *petrified.*

LAURA: That's a regular school A-minus. If I ever

went to a prep school like yours, I'd be lucky to pull C's! *(Eager to change the subject.)* Listen, I meant to tell you before. I'm *really sorry* about the scene at my house.

JEFFREY: Scene? That wasn't really a . . . scene.

LAURA: My mother always says things like that when dates come to the house.

JEFFREY: She does?

LAURA: I mean, the first *time* dates come to the house. She wouldn't do that to *you* again, if you were to— God, I'm sorry about my father.

JEFFREY: No problem.

LAURA: He just likes to be firm about things. I'm sure he didn't mean to get so . . . graphic.

JEFFREY: Hey, don't worry about it. I didn't mind at all. Your little brother's got strong fists, though. In a few years I wouldn't want to meet him in a dark alley!

LAURA: Her.

JEFFREY: What?

LAURA: Her; that's my sister Margaret.

JEFFREY: You're kidding, right? . . . Oh, boy. . . .

LAURA: It's a perfectly natural mistake; she's very masculine.

(Silence.)

LAURA: Do you think people look like their names?

JEFFREY: I guess so.

LAURA *(thoughtfully):* You don't look like a Jeffrey.

JEFFREY: No?

LAURA: No, you look like a—a James, or Timothy. *(Exuberantly.)* That's it! You look like a Timothy!

JEFFREY: A Timothy?

LAURA: Yeah.

JEFFREY *(uneasily):* What does a Timothy look like?

LAURA: Oh, tall, thin, clean-cut, kind of awkward, and— Do I look like a Laura?

JEFFREY: I couldn't say.

LAURA: Do I look like what you *thought* I was going to?

JEFFREY: Well, no.

LAURA: Really?

JEFFREY: No.

LAURA: Why? What did you think I was going to look like?

JEFFREY: Well . . .

LAURA: What did Ellis say?

JEFFREY: He said you had a nice personality.

LAURA: Yeah?

JEFFREY: He said you were fun to be with.

LAURA: What else?

JEFFREY: He said you were one of the nicest girls he knew.

LAURA: So . . .

JEFFREY *(matter-of-factly):* I thought you were a dog.

LAURA *(coughs):* Did he tell you I play tennis?

JEFFREY: No.

LAURA: Do you play tennis?

JEFFREY: No.

LAURA *(hopefully):* Soccer? I play soccer.

JEFFREY: I think I saw you on the field once.

LAURA: I knew you played soccer! I was captain this year!

JEFFREY: I was walking the dog.

LAURA: Well . . . I didn't like it that much, anyway. Do you . . . like . . . movies?

JEFFREY: Sure.

LAURA: I'm mad about them. Especially the old ones, with Bergman and Bacall. The old stars had something about them. Bette Davis could say more inhaling tobacco than most could say in years of dialogue!

JEFFREY: I go for Raquel Welch myself.

LAURA: I guess there's something about her too.

JEFFREY: Yeah, and it's got nothing to do with tobacco.

LAURA: I *love* Paul Newman.

JEFFREY: He's okay.

LAURA: And Dustin Hoffman. And— *(At this point she begins to laugh hysterically.)* —and ROBERT REDFORD!

JEFFREY: Is something funny here?

LAURA: No; it's just . . . ROBERT RED-FORD . . .

JEFFREY: What?

LAURA: ELLIS SAID YOU LOOKED LIKE HIM! *(She bursts out laughing and then shuts up abruptly.)* Well, you sort of do. *(Pause.)* I'm so glad you wore basic black.

JEFFREY: Well, I figured it was a good tux color and everything—

LAURA: Oh, it's the *only* tux color! Ellis told me you were okay, but I was terrified you might show up in something technicolor . . . banana yellow, or crushed velvet. I would've *dropped dead.*

JEFFREY *(with a nervous chuckle):* I'm glad I wore it, too, then— I mean, who wants to slab out at the prom, right?

(Silence. JEFFREY, *with some effort, pulls a small flask out from his cummerbund and tips it toward her glass. He speaks now somewhat hesitantly.)*

I brought something along to make the conversation sparkle?

LAURA: Is that a question or did you really?

JEFFREY: I did really.

LAURA *(having taken a sip):* My GOD, what *is* that?

JEFFREY: Dewar's.

LAURA: What's in it?

JEFFREY: Dewar's.

LAURA: Oh, well—I guess it is dangerous to mix drinks!

(She laughs at herself, and he returns the flask from whence it came.)

JEFFREY: So you play soccer.

LAURA: Well, yeah.

JEFFREY: You're *good* too.

LAURA: Not really.

JEFFREY: Two goals, two assists—AVERAGE—for every game? That's *good.*

LAURA: Well, it's okay. I mean, there are people a lot better than me. *(Pause.)* Hey, how did you know?

JEFFREY: Know what?

LAURA: Two goals, two assists.

JEFFREY: Oh, the newspaper. I saw your picture on the sports page.

LAURA: Oh, God—I was sweating and my shorts were too tight—

JEFFREY: And your nostrils were intimidating! *(Flares his.)*

LAURA: Oh, I just hated that coming out.

JEFFREY: Come on, it was great. . . . Is your hair different since then?

LAURA: Yeah, it's been washed.

JEFFREY: No, no, it's—I don't know . . . fluffy.

LAURA: Fluffy?

JEFFREY: Yeah—sort of like you could land something in it.

(Silence.)

LAURA: I do wish we were sitting with some other people. Not that this is *bad* or anything, but . . .

JEFFREY: I was wondering why we were alone.

LAURA: Well, to get seated with your friends you had to bring in your bid money on time; and since I didn't have a date till the last minute . . .

JEFFREY: Ellis told me you were going with your boyfriend till—

LAURA: That's right, but I hadn't brought in the money yet because I wasn't sure John would go.

JEFFREY: You weren't sure your boyfriend would take you to your *prom?*

LAURA: Well, he—he hates proms. John would've taken me, but he hates proms.

JEFFREY *(dryly):* I can't imagine why.

LAURA: He's very outdoorsy . . . and very casual, and tuxes make him itch. Not that it matters now anyway, because he's sick as a dog.

JEFFREY: What's the matter with him?

LAURA: Typhoid.

JEFFREY: Your boyfriend has TYPHOID?

LAURA *(coolly):* A mild case, yes.

JEFFREY: And you came here?

LAURA: Well, my mother made me. I'm ready to go to pieces, really, but my mother made me.

JEFFREY: Didn't she *understand?*

LAURA: She . . . doesn't like John. She doesn't like my boyfriend being so much older than me.

JEFFREY: How old is he?

LAURA: Twenty-two.

JEFFREY: Twenty-two?

LAURA: Well, he's immature.

JEFFREY: Did he go to college?

LAURA: Of course.

JEFFREY: Where?

LAURA: The—University of—Madrid.

JEFFREY: In SPAIN, Madrid?

LAURA: Yes. He has family there.

JEFFREY: How did you meet him?

LAURA: I met him—I met him at church.

JEFFREY: Church?

LAURA: Yes. He . . . had no money for the collection, and I gave him a quarter.

JEFFREY: And you've been going out ever since?

LAURA: Yes.

JEFFREY: And I'm here with you.

LAURA: You got it.

JEFFREY: Ellis told me his name was Matt.

LAURA: Who?

JEFFREY: The baseball player. He ripped his calf sliding into third. So then of course he couldn't come to the prom, and of course you needed a date, because of course you had paid all this money.

LAURA: You must admit, Ellis is creative. . . . May I have some more of that?

JEFFREY (*pulling out flask and pouring*): Be my guest.

LAURA: So, what are you majoring in?

JEFFREY: Major in chemistry, minor in German.

LAURA *(having taken a sip, smacks her lips):* German. I never liked German.

JEFFREY: You took it?

LAURA: No; I mean the way it sounds. Angry, or something.

JEFFREY: Oh, I find Germans friendly.

LAURA: How can you tell when they spit constantly? *(Exaggerated imitation.) Ach* and *ich.* Look at the way they say hello. *GUTEN TAG.* If you didn't know any better, you'd think it was "Shove it, buddy."

(Silence.)

JEFFREY: Well, you're quiet all of a sudden.

LAURA: Shock of the month.

JEFFREY: No, no . . .

LAURA: Gets on your nerves, doesn't it?

JEFFREY: No, no, not at all . . .

LAURA: Come on, Jeffrey, I *know.* I spoke my first sentence, for God's sake, and kept going. When I was three, my foot took up permanent residence in my mouth. *(Slower now.)* Yeah, I say too much. *(Beginning to babble.)* I mean, I know I do, even as I'm doing it, but I can't help it—and then after I've been blabbering on about nothing, which is what I usually do blabber on about, I feel so stupid. *(Sheepishly.)* Like now.

JEFFREY: There's really no need to feel stupid—

LAURA *(ignoring this, as if just realizing some-*

thing): Funny, isn't it? I mean, I *hate* small talk. And it's what I do best. *(Flippant again.)* If I thought half as much as I talked—

JEFFREY: You'd need years of therapy. So quit apologizing for nothing.

(Silence.)

JEFFREY: So, do you have your license yet?

LAURA: No.

JEFFREY: Do you drive?

LAURA *(morosely):* No.

JEFFREY *(after a pause):* Oh, well. It's not as great as you think it is. Having your license, I mean.

LAURA: No?

JEFFREY: You always get nailed for rides and things.

LAURA: I guess you would.

JEFFREY: You can come and go when you want, though.

LAURA: THAT would be heaven.

JEFFREY: IF you can get the car. Usually I can get my dad's old Chrysler. I think Truman was in when they got it.

LAURA: They don't make 'em like they used to.

JEFFREY: If you had my car, you'd know why. I'm not complaining, though. It's a disaster, but it gets me where I want to go. *(Pause.)* Sometimes I just take that old thing, and drive.

LAURA: By *yourself?*

JEFFREY: By myself. I just turn up the radio, turn down the windows, and *drive.*

LAURA: Why do you do that?

JEFFREY: To be alone, I guess.

LAURA: Can't you be alone without one-twenty to the gallon?

JEFFREY: Well, if I'm home I've got to be doing something. Help my dad, hit the books—anything. Get something accomplished. When you're standing still, see, there's no excuse for wasting time. But in the *car*—in the car, you can't *do* anything else. You've got your two hands on the wheel, your eyes on the road, and your head wherever you feel like putting it.

LAURA: Your head wherever you feel like putting it. I'll drink to that!

JEFFREY *(pouring):* I'm glad to see I brought your favorite.

LAURA *(solemnly):* Actually, I *don't drink.*

JEFFREY: Really.

LAURA: Oh, I sip every so often . . . but I *don't drink.*

JEFFREY: Yeah, well, some people sip more than others.

LAURA: And I only sip certain things. Champagne! Wine!

JEFFREY: Scotch straight up!

LAURA: That's this, right? Yeah, this is okay. *(Pause.)* You aren't drinking any.

JEFFREY: No, I'm not.

LAURA: Why not?

JEFFREY: It—uh—makes me stupid.

LAURA *(sadly):* Oh.

(Silence. She sinks into a sort of lull of depression.)

JEFFREY: So . . . do you have any brothers or sisters? Besides the one that attack—I, uh, met?

LAURA: One other sister.

JEFFREY: Really?

LAURA: Wendy. She's two.

JEFFREY: Oh?

LAURA: She drools a lot.

JEFFREY: Hmmm.

LAURA: She only knows two words. *Mommy* and *Fruit Loop. (Ponderously.)* I guess that counts as three words, doesn't it?

JEFFREY: I guess.

LAURA *(after a pause):* You know what bothers me about little kids?

JEFFREY: They eat with their mouths open and smell bad.

LAURA: No.

JEFFREY: *No?* They can get downright revolting. My sister Ellen—she's five now—she went through this whole thing about sticking stuff up her nose. If it could fit, in it went.

LAURA: But you know what really gets me about little kids?

JEFFREY: What?

LAURA: They're so goddamned . . . happy.

JEFFREY: They've got one hell of a nerve, the little snots.

LAURA: I'm serious. It's not even *that* they're happy; it's *why*. Take Wendy. Saturday morning, it's not even light yet—and she's busting out of her Batman jammies over Josie and the Pussycats. Give her a crayon and she'll spend the whole day, singing and drawing on herself.

JEFFREY: Ellen sings in the bath. . . .

LAURA *(with much more contempt than appropriate)*: You should see her eat an Oreo . . .

JEFFREY: She, uh, likes to run around in the buff . . .

LAURA: . . . can't do it without that goddamned song. I won't give her cookies and milk at the same time. It's *suicide*.

JEFFREY: Well . . .

LAURA: Doesn't it bother you? I mean, they're short and loud and hang up the phone on people . . . swallow nickels and put peanut butter on the dog . . . can't tell a totalitarian from a Twinkie—

JEFFREY: They're not supposed to!

LAURA: It isn't fair. It just isn't fair.

JEFFREY: What are you talking about, fair?

LAURA: Nothing, I guess— Listen, Jeffrey, would you mind if I left you alone for a minute?

JEFFREY *(smiling)*: Not at all.

LAURA *(tightly):* Then I think I'll go . . . freshen up a bit.

JEFFREY: You go ahead.

LAURA *(rising):* Don't go away.

JEFFREY: Don't worry. *(Turning his head.)* I can't.

(Exit LAURA.*)*

ACT TWO

LAURA *is returning.*

JEFFREY *has remained at the table.*

JEFFREY: Dinner was pretty good.

LAURA: I'm sorry I missed it. It wasn't my fault, though. I was held up by Mrs. Straussingheissen.

JEFFREY: Who?

LAURA: Mrs. Straussingheissen. My health teacher. Disgusting woman.

JEFFREY: Really.

LAURA *(with tipsy indignation):* She wasn't going to let me back into the prom! She said I had been drinking!

JEFFREY *(with mock astonishment):* No!

LAURA: I don't know why they had her at the door anyway, the old liver-spotted earthworm!

(Silence during which LAURA *huffs in anger and* JEFFREY *becomes nervous.)*

JEFFREY: So . . . do you want to dance?

LAURA *(dreamily):* Oh, Jeffrey, do you *dance?*

JEFFREY: Not a step, but it's got to be easier than this.

LAURA: I've been waiting for you to ask me all night.

JEFFREY: It probably wasn't worth the wait, but why not?

LAURA: Oh, I'd *love* to dance, Jeffrey, but I'm too sleepy.

JEFFREY: You're sleepy?

LAURA: No . . . but if I get up, the room might take off.

JEFFREY: You didn't drink *that* much.

LAURA: Oh, yes, I did.

JEFFREY *(almost hissing):* You drank in the *bathroom?*

LAURA: No!

JEFFREY: Thank God.

LAURA: However, on the way back . . .

JEFFREY: I don't believe it.

LAURA: I'm not that far gone, but I don't want to take any chances. I mean, you probably have to take that tux back tomorrow, and I wouldn't want to . . . get anything on it.

JEFFREY *(muttering):* I should've known . . . you smell like eighty proof Chanel. Here, have some ice cream. It'll coat your stomach.

LAURA: Is it good?

JEFFREY: It's not exactly Mom's homemade, but I don't think you'll notice.

LAURA: Does your mother make ice cream?

JEFFREY: Yeah, she does. Sometimes.

LAURA: That's so American.

JEFFREY: Just call me Davy Crockett.

LAURA: What's your favorite flavor?

JEFFREY: Vanilla.

LAURA: Vanilla! You must be a conservative.

JEFFREY: I mean, *great* vanilla. All I have to do is think of summer and I can smell great vanilla.

LAURA: I smell salt.

JEFFREY: The air at the beach?

LAURA: The stuff on my french fries . . .

JEFFREY: Just think: two more weeks till high school is mere memory.

LAURA: Until September, anyway. We're going to the shore.

JEFFREY: So are we.

LAURA: Hey, have you ever heard of Bostwick's-on-the-Boardwalk? Now, *that's* great vanilla.

JEFFREY: Heard of it? I just about live there.

LAURA: Did you ever have the Holy Moses?

JEFFREY: I tried it once, but halfway through I almost died. All that pineapple sauce.

LAURA: I polished off two in one sitting.

JEFFREY: How'd you manage that?

LAURA: Lotsa practice. . . . One of these days we ought to get together and pig out.

JEFFREY: God, I can't wait for that vacation.

LAURA: It's kind of a headache, though. I mean, have you ever been to the beach with a little kid? They're *vicious* with water and sand.

JEFFREY: Here we go again.

LAURA *(maliciously):* You know what's the worst thing you can do to a little kid at the beach?

JEFFREY: What?

LAURA: Knock down their sandcastle! I mean, they'll fry themselves alive, get eight pounds of sand in their pants, and still they sit there—piling it and molding it and patting it together. Making a moat. Thinking. And then you come along and jump in it, tear it to absolute bits. All that work, all that tender imagination—reduced to a zillion grains of plain, ordinary sand. *(Pause.)* It's a great feeling.

JEFFREY: You really do hate them, don't you?

LAURA *(wearily):* Oh, I'm just jealous.

JEFFREY *(exasperated):* WHY?

LAURA *(carelessly):* Oh, I don't know . . . *(Grandly.)* Their perpetual oblivion. That's as good a reason as any, isn't it? Per-pet-u-al oblivion. They like everything, believe everything—then they get to grammar school, and that's the end of that.

JEFFREY: Okay, so you find out Walt Disney isn't God. You can't find the Answer to Life in a box of Coco Puffs. It's not exactly the end of the world.

LAURA *(pointedly):* I'm just not that eager to get out of school this year, okay, Jeffrey?

JEFFREY: The idea of summer does not excite you at *all?*

LAURA: Oh, I'm shaking all over. How about you?

JEFFREY: Yes!

LAURA: Why?

JEFFREY: Because the commencement of summer conversely entails the conclusion of academic pursuits during an interval commonly referred to as vacation. You know, "no more pencils, no more books"? Laura, the last day of school is like having been in a cage all year and then watching the wires snap.

LAURA *(sarcastically):* What do you do once they free you, Jeffrey? Climb on cars at Jungle Habitat?

JEFFREY: Nothing, Laura; I just do *nothing*.

LAURA: Really? No cancer research for the next couple of weeks?

JEFFREY: Oh, boy.

LAURA: What?

JEFFREY: It's about to happen. I can smell it.

LAURA: What?

JEFFREY: Just say what you were going to say.

LAURA: I simply thought, Jeffrey, that with your brains—

JEFFREY: THERE IT IS!

LAURA *(jumps in her seat)*: What?

JEFFREY: The dreaded skeleton in my closet: brains!

LAURA: Are you telling me you're ashamed of your intelligence?

JEFFREY: No, just not proud of it.

LAURA: Don't be ridiculous.

JEFFREY: Are you proud of having ten toes?

LAURA: Of course not.

JEFFREY: Why not?

LAURA: I was *born* with—

JEFFREY: There it is. Why be proud of something I had nothing to do with?

LAURA: Be real. You talk about an IQ as if it's a disease.

JEFFREY: Some guys have athlete's foot; I have—

LAURA: Brains?

JEFFREY: Of course, brains. What are we talking about here?

LAURA: Jeffrey, I don't think it's right to compare

your intelligence with—with the fungus on the bottom of some jock's foot. Don't tell me it's no advantage to be smart.

JEFFREY: An advantage, sure. But it's not *righteous!* Think about it. I could be the worst sleaze on the face of the earth, and it'd be okay because of my almighty SAT's.

LAURA: I don't want to sound nosy or anything, but—how good are your grades? I mean, are they *obscenely* high?

JEFFREY: You know how you get good grades, Laura? You tell 'em what they want to hear, and you tell 'em in a vocabulary they don't understand. *That's* the big secret.

LAURA: I'm sorry. I just assumed—

JEFFREY: Don't be sorry. Everybody assumes everything about everybody else, and they're always wrong. It's how we get through life.

(Silence.)

LAURA *(getting up):* Oh, they're crowning the prom queen. I wonder who it is?

JEFFREY: I can't see either. I think she's blond, though.

LAURA *(after a pause):* It was really nice of you to come, Jeffrey.

JEFFREY: Oh, it's my pleasure.

LAURA: I know it was very last minute, and you're great for doing it.

JEFFREY: Well, I'm having a good time.

LAURA: Oh, you don't have to say that.

JEFFREY: I'm not just saying that. I'm having a good time—not great, but good.

LAURA: I'm glad. A little surprised, but glad.

JEFFREY: Why are you surprised? Aren't you enjoying yourself?

LAURA *(eagerly):* Oh, I am! I just didn't think you were.

JEFFREY: What gave you that idea?

LAURA: Well, you know, I'm not the kind of girl that— *(Breathes in, then gives a small smile as she speaks.)* I'm not exactly Raquel Welch.

JEFFREY: True.

LAURA *(ignoring this):* I'm sure you know a lot of people who are more together; like, more sophisticated than I am. Everybody says I'm young for my age.

JEFFREY: Please don't do this to yourself.

LAURA *(casually, but conveying her insecurity):* One of these days I'm going to be so gorgeous and so successful nobody in this room will recognize me. *(Chuckling, but with a slight bite to it.)* Dream on, Laura—

JEFFREY: WOULD YOU QUIT PUTTING YOURSELF THROUGH THE BLENDER? You're annoying me!

LAURA: I'm sorry.

JEFFREY: And stop it with the apologies, would you please? I'm surprised you haven't choked on them yet!

LAURA: Okay, okay! *(Slight pause.)* I know what you're thinking.

JEFFREY: This I've got to hear.

LAURA: You're thinking, "I can't believe Ellis put me up to this." You're thinking you can't wait to get this thing over with, and get the tux off, and . . . watch David Letterman. And tell your friends about this tomorrow night. I am no fool, Jeffrey. I know what reality is.

JEFFREY: You have no CONTACT with reality!

LAURA: Tell me about it. You know what reality is? Reality is knowing that just to find an ESCORT— not even a date, just someone to be *seen* with you— you have to dig somebody out from under a rock. And when that didn't work, you had to find a *friend* to dig *for* you. You know how that feels?

JEFFREY: Would you calm down?

LAURA: It feels *lousy,* Jeffrey. REALLY LOUSY.

JEFFREY: It's a high-school prom, for cryin' out loud! What's the worst thing that could have happened? You'd have spent tonight attacking your little sister! I'd feel sorry for her, not you!

LAURA *(breathing hard, almost shuddering):* No, Jeffrey. The worst thing that could have happened already did. The worst thing is the questions—questions I ask myself, day in and day out. "Am I fat?" "Am I ugly?" "Do I have any acne I didn't know about?" OR—try this one on for size—is it ME? And there's no diet, and no astringent, and no mouthwash that can help me. I'm too far gone for that! What I need is a new personality. Where do I find the catalog for that? Try it sometime, Jeff. It tickles.

JEFFREY *(slowly):* You are really, honest-to-God, certifiably nuts!

LAURA: SO THAT'S WHAT SCARES 'EM OFF!

JEFFREY: You know what you are, Laura? You are greedy.

LAURA: That's a new one.

JEFFREY: Yeah, it's a new one. You want everything. You want cover-girl bone structure, and thighs you could wrap a pinky around twice, and one of those perky party personalities so you can be popularity queen of the world! And then you want to get into every school with ivy crawling up it, and you want to kick the soccer ball from here to Helsinki. You don't just *want* perfection, Laura, you feel CHEATED without it!

LAURA *(swallowing hard):* YOU—

JEFFREY: FACE IT. You're not Cheryl Tiegs and Helen Keller rolled into one. Well, you're not a martyr, either, so stop acting so goddamned put-upon.

LAURA: Shut up, Jeffrey.

JEFFREY: Fine.

LAURA: Let me tell you a thing or two. You don't know what it's like. You don't have to sit around waiting for somebody—

JEFFREY: Neither do you!

LAURA: What are you talking about?

JEFFREY: I'm talking about Dating. The Dating

Game. It's a canceled game show, not your *life,* for God's sake! What goes through your head? A guy is a guy. He's human. He breathes. He's probably got a few disgusting habits. But you act as if you haven't got a right arm until you find some schmuck to take you out—and then you feel lucky he'd give you the time of day, because you don't think you deserve any better. No wonder you come on like a cold salami on rye. You set yourself up for your own misery. *(Resigned.)* Well, drown in it.

LAURA *(meekly):* Can we leave now?

JEFFREY: And you know why little kids are so goddamned happy, as you so poetically put it?

LAURA: I don't care—

JEFFREY: Because they haven't got a checklist for what they're supposed to be. How *can* you be happy with a mirror to your face twenty-four hours a day? How can you look at anything when you're so busy looking at yourself and taking potshots at what you see?

(Her head is trembling visibly.)

JEFFREY *(panicked):* Oh, God, don't cry . . . don't! . . . You're crying. I made her cry. *(Pause. Then softly pleading.)* Listen, I didn't mean it. I—I was only making conversation. Here, wipe your nose.

(She does not take the napkin he offers her.)

LAURA: They'll charge me for the linen.

JEFFREY: Come on, stop crying. People are going to pass us on the way out; they'll think I hit you. *(Desperately.)* Have some ice cream. You never finished your ice cream . . . Please? *(Raises spoon, as if to feed a baby.)* Comin' down and it's headin' for the tunnel . . . chug-a-chug-a-chug-a CHOO! CHOO! *(Glob of ice cream slides off spoon as it stops short in front of her tightly closed mouth.)*

LAURA *(reacting spontaneously)*: ACH—

JEFFREY: Oh, God. Now all I have to do is make you walk home.

(LAURA begins to laugh hysterically.)

JEFFREY: You're laughing? No, you're crying . . . no, I was right. You're laughing. Does the word *schizo* mean anything to you?

LAURA: This is the worst night of my life!

JEFFREY: You make a lot of sense.

LAURA: Warm vanilla is trickling down my abdomen. I cannot talk sense, Jeffrey.

JEFFREY: I'll have it cleaned.

LAURA: You are a piece of work . . . the only person I know who'll tear someone to shreds and then come out with "I'll have it cleaned."

JEFFREY: Okay, clean it yourself.

(They laugh.)

LAURA: Well, this has been interesting.

JEFFREY: That's safe to say.

LAURA *(after a thoughtful pause):* Jeffrey? Are you scared?

JEFFREY: What is that supposed to—

LAURA: Are you?

JEFFREY *(surprised by his own answer):* Yeah.

LAURA: I'm scared of the future.

JEFFREY: So is the rest of the world.

LAURA *(carefully):* I'm scared of getting to the future and finding out that none of it is ever real.

JEFFREY: None of what?

LAURA: None of this—preparation. You're young, you spend your whole life looking *forward* to something. What if it's nothing? It really could be nothing, Jeffrey—like reading a brochure that says you're going to Paradise, and you wind up in the Holiday Inn. THE FUTURE, the great, perfect future. It's probably a lot of days, exactly like the ones we have now. And I'll spend all this time, running and rushing and cramming and making a good impression . . . and then one morning I'll wake up and see how dumb it was—how dumb *I* was—and I'll be the butt of this very obvious joke.

JEFFREY: Sometimes, when I'm stuck in the books —I mean, really crazy memorizing all those laws of chemistry and physiology—I get to thinking, This could all collapse. Some guy could come along and *disprove* the stuff to pieces. Make an idiot of Einstein and me both. And then what's all that agony going to be worth?

LAURA: Not a hill of beans, Jeffrey.

JEFFREY: But you know what the one great thing is?

LAURA: What?

JEFFREY: I don't care.

LAURA: What?

JEFFREY: I don't give a damn. I can't. *You* can't. Nobody can. Who'd spend sixty bucks for chicken croquettes and a table in Siberia? Who'd stick a shrub on her wrist and try to be Lauren Bacall? Who'd get anything done if they had to make sure it had *meaning* all the time?

LAURA: You know, you're right.

JEFFREY: Listen, I really feel bad about . . .

LAURA: What?

JEFFREY: Attacking you.

LAURA: Jeffrey, you haven't touched me all night.

JEFFREY: Verbally, I mean.

LAURA: Don't give it another thought.

JEFFREY: I only said it because—well, you've got a lot going for you, and you shouldn't swallow it so much.

LAURA: I got the message.

JEFFREY: I guess you did.

LAURA: Loud and clear.

JEFFREY *(after a pause):* Sounds like they're doing the last dance . . . ? *(There is a hesitant invitation in his voice, to which they both wag their heads no.)* Well, then, I guess I'd better go find our coats.

LAURA *(slightly disappointed):* Okay—have you got the tickets?

JEFFREY: I think so. *(Rises.)* I'll be right back. *(Starts to leave, then turns around.)* Hey—maybe we could find a Holy Moses someplace . . . without the pineapple sauce.

LAURA: I think I'd wear that well.

(Exit JEFFREY. LAURA, *visibly brightened, picks up her still half-filled glass and looks at it for a second. Deciding to drink it, she gives an oh-why-not facial expression.)*

Here's to you, Ellis.

CURTAIN

PATRICIA DURKIN

At this point my "biography" is a lot of empty space waiting to be filled. The youngest of seven, I have lived in the same New Jersey house my whole life. I am interested in most things (except mathematics) and find that inquiry of any kind can turn itself back into writing of whatever form it wants to take—an essay, short story, or dialogue. Work in each of these areas only solidifies work in the others.

Since the staging of *Fixed Up* I have spent a summer in Strasbourg, France, and then a fall, winter, and spring at Yale, where I have done more reading than writing. Exposure to characters both between book covers and on the street has proven a real outing for my imagination but has left me at a loss on the question of the future. I hope it includes a pen in some essential spot, but my life changes faces more often than I change my sheets, so I am unqualified to comment.

About the Play

The Young Playwrights Festival always struck me as being fictional. I kept waiting for the odd quality of winning to rub off, but it never did. Instead, it expanded into the equally strange and lovely sensation of entering a world at once unknown and hospitable: Theater. It was real, I knew, but it never became quite plausible.

As a title, *Festival* is apt, for it hints at unreality. Like all pleasant exceptions—surprises and holidays—it is giddy and fantastic and filled with its own sense of being temporary. Even before it begins, there is regret for the moment when it will end. Like the best ride in the park, it is a taut wait, a decadent spin, an abrupt halt. A touch of vertigo. The giddiness fools itself, for a while, that it is still in motion, and lingers a little before it goes away.

A year of hindsight yields the glorious postscript: It is not missed. There is no time to pine after old graces. There is too much work. At the Festival *work* is freed from being a dishpan word, constantly begging to be interrupted. In theater, work is an interaction from which a fool would want to be distracted. It is concentration and energy and creation. It is the greatest fun, the grittiest satisfaction, the finest memory. It is the one rule less predictable than any exception. And unlike any piece of luck, work never runs out. The Festival offers a fine foreshadowing of what is real in theater. The variables change, but the process continues. Work provides the constant to which I can return, the temptation to try it again.

THIRD STREET

by Richard Colman
(age eighteen when play was written)

CHARACTERS

Ronnie
John
Frankie

An abandoned Brooklyn graveyard.

It is twilight. The tombstones are old and faded and crowded together. In the distance we can see elevated train tracks.

There are a few six-packs of beer on one of the tombstones, and three youths are leaning or sitting on tombstones. It is the summer after they have graduated from high school. They have been friends since their earliest memories.

RONNIE seems to lead the group's thought. They work in the neighborhood and come to the graveyard to get away from their houses, their families, and Brooklyn in general. On the nice afternoons they used to cut school to sit and talk and get high. The cemetery is a private place for them. Once in a while somebody's girl tags along, but this is distinctly their spot. An especially prominent tombstone stands at center stage. They have put graffiti on it for years. They can trace their history on it.

As the scene opens, RONNIE is leaning against a grave marker; he is cleaning and rolling dope. He enjoys this activity and puts a lot of care into it. JOHN is seated with his back to the audience; he stares out toward the train tracks. FRANKIE is seated on a large headstone; he is drinking beer.

The pace is slow throughout the beginning minutes. There is no rush to say anything, because the three friends have played this scene before, in years of minor variations.

RON: Nice dope . . . really nice.
JOHN *(distantly):* Yeah. Yeah, it's good.
FRANK: It's not bad. I took it from my brother.

(He laughs.)

My brother! In junior high school! Remember how afraid we used to be we'd get caught when we used to go out in the backyard to get high? It's funny, y'know? I mean, it's just kinda funny.

JOHN: Yeah, that was funny. What were we so nervous we were gonna get caught for?

FRANK: I dunno. I just thought I shouldn't encourage little Tony, y'know? He's still kinda little, right? So I figure it's in his best interest to steal his dope.

(A smile lights up his face. He loves this story. When he tells it, JOHN and RONNIE pretend that they have never heard it—or perhaps they really don't remember it that well. In any case, they love to hear old stories.)

Remember . . . Remember . . . Remember when . . .

(FRANKIE bursts out laughing just thinking about it. The beer and dope add to the quality and duration of everybody's laughter.)

JOHN: What is it, Frankie? Huh? Spit it out!

(The laughter builds until at the end of the story they can barely breathe.)

FRANK: Remember—

(He is constantly going off on laughing jags that infect JOHN *and* RONNIE.)

Remember after ninth-grade graduation, we snuck over to that storage shed in Rosen's backyard to get stoned? And we're sitting there smoking away, and Rosen's dad sees all that smoke comin' out the crack by the door? And he calls the fire department and we hear those sirens comin' from way off and Ronnie says "They're comin' to get us," and you said, "Don't be so paranoid," and the sirens just keep getting closer and closer, and we hear them pull up in the driveway! And we're all peeing in our pants! And we ate all the dope we had left! And the firemen pull open those doors and they're standing there with that! That hose! And we're just sitting there in the dark, out of our minds!

(The laughter lasts a long time.)

JOHN: That was so funny!

RON: You didn't think so at the time.

JOHN: I didn't think it was so funny! Man, you should've seen your face, your eyes was like a frog!

RON: Man, you were trying to burrow under those rusty old beach chairs!

FRANK: I was pretty cool about the whole thing.

*(RONNIE *and* JOHN *laugh.)*

JOHN: Oh, yeah, real cool except for that big dump you took in your pants!

FRANK: You're full of it!

RON: Oh, come off it, Frankie, saying your Hail Marys is not exactly an indication of cool!

(They all laugh.)

FRANK: I guess I was a little nervous. . . . We thought they were gonna lock us up for life. *(Reading tombstone.)* "Rosen's garage. June twenty-eighth, 1979." What was that—three, four years ago? Doesn't seem that long.

JOHN: Nice dope.

FRANK: Yeah. My brother gets better grass than I do. 'Course, he gets an allowance.

(They begin to laugh again, but it passes more quickly. Silence for a while.)

Got me a vacation comin' up in two weeks.

RON: Still goin' down to Florida?

FRANK: Nah. Gonna stay home and lie out on the porch. Use the money I'll save to put in one of those aboveground pools, y'know. For Tony and Rocco's little friends. Right in the backyard so they don't have to go all the way down to Coney Island so my ma don't have to worry.

JOHN: Nice. . . . When I get me a house I'm gonna put one of those in for sure.

FRANK: I'm taking it on time payments—it's real cheap.

RON: Real cheap for a looong time.

(They laugh.)

FRANK *(just slightly annoyed, more defensive):* It's gonna be nice, though.

(They are quiet. FRANKIE plucks a beer. They smoke some more. JOHN lights a cigarette. The quiet lasts maybe fifteen seconds, maybe thirty. They are taking care of the business of getting their brains into a condition they feel comfortable in. Then FRANKIE speaks for no apparent reason.)

Hey, Mr. Cohen! You're so fat that if you had four wheels, you could be a truck!

(At first JOHN and RONNIE are caught off guard. Then they remember and laugh! laugh! laugh!)

JOHN *(still laughing):* Remember when you said that to Mr. Cohen during that final exam—I thought I'd bust a gut! That was so funny!

(The laughter passes. There is quiet. They continue to smoke dope. Suddenly FRANKIE starts to giggle—a little at first. Then he begins to laugh harder and harder till he's rolling on the floor. JOHN and RONNIE start to giggle, too, till they're all laughing hard. It fades. It starts up again for a second and finally passes. Some moments pass.)

FRANK *(takes a beer; he has asked RONNIE this question before):* So—when's that college start?

RON: Twenty-third of August. Leave in about a week and a half.

FRANK: What's that school of yours called again? Flintstone?

RON: Princeton.

FRANK: Ohh.

JOHN (odd tone): Sign up for classes?

RON: Yeah, usual boring stuff. Math, English . . .

FRANK: Huhh.

(Everyone is getting more and more stoned. FRANKIE bursts out laughing again.)

Remember—at graduation—when you won that math award or something, me and John and that geek Millman started that chant for you? (Mimicking an old teacher.) "And the winner of the 1982 Nathaniel Phipps Mathematics Award is . . . Ronald Crane!"

(FRANK and JOHN begin the chant, softly at first, then building.)

Crane the brain, Crane the brain, Crane the Brain, Crane the Brain, Crane the Brain, CRANE THE BRAIN!

(JOHN and FRANKIE are hysterical. RON is not amused, though he pretends to be.)

FRANK: Man, everyone was doin' it!

RON: No, it wasn't everyone.

JOHN: Aw, g'wan, we must've had at least twenty people.

FRANK: Anyone that mattered, anyway.

RON *(blurts it out):* My parents felt really retarded.

(JOHN and FRANKIE continue to laugh, though not as hard. They refuse to notice when RONNIE won't partake in group jokes. Silence for a while. They drink and smoke and gather strength.)

So, Frankie, what's it gonna be? You gonna stay on at Mario's Primo Meats, or what? When you gotta let him know?

FRANK: Yeah, I figure I'll do him a favor and stay on there. I got the payments to keep up on the Corvette. Probably stay there till something better comes along. My dad's old boss says all the time, "Maybe soon, maybe soon I get a job for you in the garage." The old liar.

JOHN: He owes it to you, all the time your dad put in there.

FRANK: Lot more'n a job he owes my family. My dad was an institution. Anyway, I kinda like the butcher business.

RON: Beats office work any day of the week.

JOHN *(suddenly):* You know what I was thinking about this morning at work? I was lifting those forty-pound boxes of loose-leaf paper for that Greenbaum and I got to thinkin' about how we always used to say we were going to take off in a van right after high school and go see something. Just scout around, check out America.

FRANK: Hey, maybe we can go next year.

JOHN: Yeah, for two weeks in July. It's different for you, you got your family at home to support. Me, I got nothin'.

FRANK: Hey, don't say that, John, you got Elise.

JOHN: I got too much Elise.

(They all laugh nervously.)

FRANK: When'd she get so fat?

JOHN: Pregnant, you jerk, not fat!

RON: The minute they get married, they expand anyway. Like all the tension is just released! Sure, being married's got its good points—you're getting laid whenever you want!

(They all laugh.)

FRANK: When's the kid due?

JOHN: I dunno, couple of months. Elise is like a beached whale around the house. Whining and groaning. Jesus Christ, it could make ya puke! "Get me this, get me that." She's all right, though.

RON: She's a nice girl.

FRANK: Yeah, she's real nice.

JOHN: Like a beached whale. Like deadweight.

FRANK: Gonna be a good-looking kid, your kid. Nice kid. I'm gonna be the godfather—me and Ronnie. You can leave him with us anytime you want to go somewhere with Elise.

JOHN: She's always sittin' around watchin' TV and eatin'.

FRANK: She's supposed to eat a lot, she's eatin' for two.

JOHN: She's eatin' for twenty!

(Nervous laughter.)

Like an infantry unit. The kid's gonna come out a middleweight, for chrissakes!

FRANK *(as if trying to make it true by saying it):* You can't fool me, I know you love her.

JOHN: Oh, yeah, we're married; don't get me wrong, she's a great girl. It's just that sometimes I feel like I need her, sometimes I can't stand to look at her. Sometimes I feel like I know her, but sometimes I feel like I could leave her ten thousand miles behind and forget her name by the time I passed Newark.

RON: When I found out she was pregnant, I thought, Wow, that's terrific.

FRANK: Yeah, definitely, it's like we're all gonna be one big family, y'know? It's gonna be real cool! Picnics!! Cub Scouts! Zoos! Bring him up to college to see Uncle Ronnie! You're gonna be tops in the pops department!

JOHN *(suddenly):* Maybe I'll go up to school with you for a while. I wouldn't bother you. Maybe I could just get an apartment and see you once in a while after classes. We could catch a movie . . .

(FRANKIE *laughs nervously.*)

Then Frankie could come up. We could get jobs while you study, and then when the summertime rolls around, we could drop a down payment on a customized van and take off!

FRANK: For points unknown!

JOHN: Yeah, what do you say?

RON (*laughs*): Oh, yeah, all of us and that kid, and Elise.

JOHN: But . . . Oh, God . . . forget about them.

(*He laughs.*)

God.

(FRANKIE *laughs.*)

FRANK: My ma said I was the man of the house now, and you got that kid to bring up. Adults like us, man, we don't go running around in no van—no way! For us, it's total and complete luxury. One-year cruise down to the Bahamas! Puerto Rico! Las Vegas! Anything, man!

JOHN: But a customized van . . .

RON: Sounds real good, John.

FRANK: Yeah, and when you're a big hotshot college graduate, you'll fly us down in your plane, private jet, and we'll parachute right onto the beach!

(*Long silence.*)

JOHN *(ever so slightly accusative):* What are you going to do about Diana?

RON: What about her?

JOHN: Gonna marry her?

RON: Nah. Don't think so. She's working at that office. In downtown, near Wall Street. Probably write her when I get to school.

FRANK: Wanta have space on that social calendar for those rich women, huh?

RON: Damn right!

JOHN *(laughs nervously):* How long's it been, you've been seeing Diana? Like ninth grade or something?

RON: Yeah. *(To* JOHN.*)* Remember the first time I did it to her? It was at that party at your house—in your parents' bedroom under all those coats piled up.

FRANK *(smiling incredulously):* You did it there? Under all those coats? On his parents' bed?

RON: Yeah!

JOHN: I think I remember that party. Jeez. I didn't realize you did it that long ago.

RON: Yeah, I did. *(Pause.)* She's all right. It's just, y'know, compatibility. We're just not compatible.

JOHN: Yeah. I kinda like her, though. She's real pleasant.

RON: Yeah, she is.

JOHN: I remember in fifth grade I once loaned her these crayons for this art project she was doing. A big box of sixty-four with a sharpener and everything. She was drawing this big house with, like, ten thousand windows on it. And all these people in the windows smiling out. And she was gonna color all the people all different colors. And she was so happy, man, when I said I'd loan her my crayons. I couldn't believe it. She was so nice. Real nice.

RON: Yeah, I like her too.

JOHN *(almost on the offensive):* How come you're so mean to her sometimes?

RON: Hey, what's the problem?

JOHN: You should be nice to her, she really likes you.

RON: Yeah, yeah.

FRANK *(senses a confrontation):* My brother said the craziest thing at dinner today—

JOHN *(cuts him off):* You asshole! She cares about you!

RON *(with implication):* Hey, you don't have to marry a girl just 'cause you lay her, you know.

JOHN: I don't know what's with you, Ronnie. You think you're some kind of hotshot. A real god— *(He grabs* RONNIE *by his shirt and hauls him to his feet.)*

RON *(overlapping from "You think you're"):* Hey, calm down, John. Don't get all worked up.

JOHN: I'm just saying be nice to her. That's all—be nice . . .

RON: Yeah, I'm nice. I am nice. We're all a bunch of nice guys, remember?

FRANK: Hey, wanna do some shots? Whaddaya say, John? You wanna do some shots?

JOHN *(softly):* No. No, thanks. Hey, I'm sorry.

(Silence.)

FRANK: You're not mad, are you, John? Ronnie didn't mean nothin' by it.

JOHN: No, really, it's all right. I'm all right. I'm sorry.

RON: John, all I meant to say was—

JOHN: I gotta go. I gotta go call Elise. She said to call, tell her where I am. I gotta go.

(He darts off. Silence. RONNIE is on the ground; FRANKIE is perched on a tombstone. Frankie's bottle is on the ground. RONNIE surveys the sky.)

RON: Nice Saturday night.

RON: Yeah.

FRANK: Hand me the bottle.

(RONNIE hands him the bottle.)

Thanks.

(He drinks and chases with a beer. He smacks his lips.)

Good.

(He hands the bottle back down.)

RON: We should've went with John to the phone. It's a long walk.

FRANK: Nah. . . . Elise just gets lonely, tells John to come home early. She drinks, y'know. Even though she's preggo.

RON *(changing the subject):* You learning anything in that butcher shop of yours?

FRANK: I'm learnin' a lot. There's a lot more to the butcher business than just hacking away.

RON: I'm sure.

FRANK: Last week I learned how to chain-saw an entire cow. They come in practically whole, and we just keep cuttin' 'em into smaller and smaller pieces. It's cool—makes me feel like a madman murderer or somethin'.

(They laugh.)

Sometimes I get to feelin' a little sad, like Old McDonald's farm's all dead. Like Old McDonald just couldn't make the payments on his Corvette and he had to sell off his little farm friends. Mostly it's cool, though—and the refrigerator place we work in is better than air-conditioning. Gonna learn that business good.

RON: Definitely.

FRANK: My sister, Marianne? She's graduating in two years from high school. Says she wants to go to college. I want to pay, y'know?

RON *(nods his head):* That's great.

FRANK: Everything's gonna be different when you're gone, man.

RON: It's different anyway. School's over and all.

FRANK: Hope you come back once in a while.

RON: I will, you know I will.

FRANK: You get off Christmas, Thanksgiving and

everything. It's just that John, he's gonna miss you. A lot, man. You don't know how much. You . . . You'll be all right, but John . . . he needs you.

RON: He'll be all right. It'll be good for him.

FRANK: 'Course, it'll be good for him. Good man. Gets up five-thirty every morning, six days a week, to toss those heavy boxes around for old Greenbaum. Plus his kid. I think it'll be good for him . . . make him, you know, grow up.

RON: I think so.

FRANK: Said he was gonna name the baby Ronald after you.

RON: No kidding.

(Pause.)

FRANK: Even if it's a girl. (FRANKIE *laughs.*) You got to be more understanding with him, Ronnie, he really respects you.

RON: Yeah, I know.

(FRANKIE *looks as if he might say something, but doesn't.)*

FRANK: I don't know. You got to write John once in a while.

RON: Sure.

FRANK: You can skip me, but John—

RON: Yeah, I will, I said.

FRANK: I never told you this before—now, I'm sure it's nothing weird, but . . . in a way, he sort of loves you.

RON: Yeah, I know there's nothing weird.

FRANK: Right, it's just that he needs you . . . like . . . sort of a role model, y'know?

RON: No, I know. Right. Definitely.

FRANK: He loves you in a positive way and he needs your support, so sometimes you have to set him straight. Hey—how'd that visit to your school go? How's it look?

RON: Nice. Big. Scary. Cool.

FRANK: Got ivy?

RON: Yeah, it's the real thing. They're not just screwin' around.

FRANK: Sure.

RON: You know, I was thinking, maybe I'd take Chinese.

FRANK: Chinese? What for?

RON: I don't know, why not? It would be cool to speak it.

FRANK: *Chingfang shaw maitai ling shoooo.* You gotta get that singsong voice down. That's the tricky part. If you can get that part, the rest of it should be a snap. It's just like the whole thing is a song, you gotta have that kind of voice, y'know?

RON: Yeah.

FRANK: Probably be easy for a smart guy like you.

RON: Maybe I'll even go over to China for a while.

FRANK: No kidding? When?

RON: Maybe a year from now.

FRANK: Wow. We'll miss you.

RON: I'll send you some jade or something.

FRANK: Send me a geisha. Yeah. Wow. That's some faraway place.

RON: Yeah, I figure it'll be a change of pace.

FRANK: Yeah, like culture differences, right. Customs and stuff. . . . Uhhh, I wasn't supposed to tell you this, but John is having this going-away dinner for you. I mean, I just thought I'd tell you so when he asks, you'll know.

RON: Yeah, sure. That'll be great.

FRANK: It's his first big party as man of the house —he's definitely doin' it up big. Bought champagne, fancy pastries, everything.

RON: Yeah, sure. Definitely.

FRANK: Elise's mom's comin' over, too, 'cause Elise doesn't cook so hot yet. Big fat thing, isn't she?

RON: She is not an individual, she's a group! *(Slight pause.)* Think Elise'll be like that someday?

FRANK: Nah. No way. . . . Couldn't be. Although she's kinda wide . . .

RON: She's got the frame.

FRANK: Sometimes I think John's not too crazy about her. You ought to tell him what a great girl she is, why it's great he married her right away.

RON: I try.

(There is the sound of a train moving over the tracks. It gets louder and louder. Frankie's next line is understandable but partially masked by the passing train.)

FRANK: Johnnie said he loved you more than anybody in the world.

(A long pause as the train recedes.)

RON: There's definitely nothing faggy about us, y'know . . . I hope you know that.
FRANK: Nobody said that, don't be an idiot. Shut up. Forget about it. Shut up.

(Each one thinks for a moment, Is John gay? Time passes. They cannot speak.)

RON: Why did he have to marry that stupid drunken can of garbage Elise, anyway?

(Silence. There is nothing to say.)

What time is it?
FRANK: Nine-seventeen.
RON: Hey—when'd you get the digital watch?
FRANK: Birthday. My little brother. Check it out. *(He shows it proudly.)* Got a lot of functions, but I don't use 'em. Hey . . . I hope we don't change too much.

(JOHN reenters.)

Löwenbräu! Now all we need's the yacht.

(JOHN is a little too quick and cheerful and bright throughout the scene.)

JOHN: Only the best for my friends. I'm a lucky guy.

FRANK: Hey, we're all lucky, we're all real lucky. We're all doin' all right. How's Elise?

JOHN: Oh, she's fine. Can't wait for me to get home. She's so horny, she's rubbin' up against the furniture. She makes me call her when I'm at work, too, just to hear my voice.

FRANK: Keep it up, man. *(He laughs.)*

JOHN: Yeah.

RON: You know, I was on the subway home today. I saw this old guy dressed real snappy, and I remembered the magic act we used to do.

JOHN: I remember, man, we used to put on that clown makeup, and I did that juggling, and that rope trick. That was an amazing rope trick.

FRANK: Yeah, and Irving the Dove? Poor Irving the Dove. Had to die. Christ, that was fun.

JOHN: Man—you never told me how you did that rope trick. Come on, how'd you do it?

(RONNIE smiling, not telling.)

I mean, I don't see any way possible you could've done that, because I remember inspecting the ropes before and after. Come on, spill, how'd you do it—?

RON: Which trick? Which of my tricks are we talkin' about?

JOHN: You know what trick I'm talkin' about—the one with the three ropes. How the hell did you do it?

RON: Come here.

(Motions to JOHN *to come closer so* FRANKIE *can't hear. Whispers something in his ear.)*

JOHN: Hmmm. Wow.

FRANK: So? How'd he do it?

JOHN: Says it was really magic. . . . I saw Janie at the superette.

RON: Janie who?

JOHN: Janie Quinn, she was in our bio class; she had long black hair, lotsa makeup, nice butt.

RON: How's she doin'?

JOHN: She's great.

RON: I know she's great; I mean how's she doin'?

JOHN: She's workin' at an office in downtown Brooklyn. Filing and typing. I took her phone number.

FRANK: I think her little sister comes over to play with my little brother.

JOHN: She ain't got no little sister. Don't you think she's pretty, Ron?

RON: Yeah, she's pretty.

JOHN: Maybe I'll give her a call sometime. No, Ronnie, you should give her a call. She remembers you. She was asking about you.

RON: Nah.

JOHN: Why not?

(Tries to force number on RONNIE.*)*

I thought she would be good enough for you, at least for a little date, like a movie or something. You can even borrow my car and take her in the back. It'll be easy to clean up, too, I got vinyl seats. Here, take it.

RON: No, what would I say to her?

FRANK: Go on, you idiot, take it, you'll think of something.

RON *(laughing)*: Yeah, I guess I will; let me have it.

JOHN: No, no, I think you were right, you really wouldn't have anything to say.

RON: Gimme it.

JOHN: Yeah, my cousin's coming in from Cleveland next weekend—

RON: Come on!

JOHN: Frankie! Frankie, you want Janie's number?

RON: John, please—I'm begging you.

JOHN: All right, here you go. . . . Enjoy.

(RONNIE *smiles when he receives it;* JOHN *smiles in response and then* FRANKIE.)

FRANK: I propose a toast. To three friends whose friendship can never end. Just like the Three Musketeers. Brave. Gallant. Gorgeous. Only cooler! May their friendship last longer than any pair of Levi's—and may they live to see many more stitches.

(They clink beer bottles.)

JOHN: Hey, Frankie, do you think now would be a good time to ask him?

FRANK: Yeah, sure. Go ahead.

JOHN: You want to come to dinner next Saturday at my place?

RON: Yeah, sure—Elise is gonna cook?

JOHN: Yeah. Her mother's coming over too. She's a regular sideshow attraction. Got a voice like an ambulance siren.

(They all laugh.)

RON: Yeah, it should be a good time. What time on Saturday?

JOHN: Seven.

RON *(suddenly remembers):* Next Saturday? Oh, God. I've got my Princeton alumni dinner I have to go to next Saturday. Oh, man. I'm sorry. Man, I'm sorry.

FRANK: Hey . . . no problem . . . it's no big deal . . . right, John? Just a little dinner and a little talk.

RON: What about another night?

JOHN: Nah. Don't worry about it. Don't worry about it. Look, I gotta be gettin' home. Elise wanted me to help her move some furniture up from the basement. I gotta go. Look, gimme a call before you leave if you can.

(JOHN runs off.)

FRANK: Hey, Flintstone. You gotta go.

(Silence.)

RON: Hey—you wanna get out of here? Let's go get Kate and Diana and go see a movie?
FRANK: Sure.
RON: Let's move.
FRANK: Hey, wait a minute. Hold on a second.

(He takes out a big black Magic Marker. He writes something on the center tombstone that has all the writing on it.)

RON: What did you write this time?
FRANK: Just the date.

(They leave slowly, walking toward the train tracks. Lights dim and out.)

END

RICHARD COLMAN

I was raised in Brooklyn and graduated from Dartmouth in 1984. At college I had a senior fellowship and won a 1985 Reynolds fellowship to go to Europe and write. I am working on my book "The Fish and the Axe," now. My hobbies are insane people and finding patterns. I was unpopular in high school. I plan to go to the New York University drama school in 1986.

About the Play

Third Street was written in one afternoon. I did it in the commons room of my dorm during the winter of 1982. The story had been on my mind for a while, but there was no particular inspiration to write it at the time. To be honest, I was probably avoiding writing a term paper. I finished by dinnertime and stuffed it into my desk. Several weeks later I typed it up and sent it off to Gerald Chapman, who'd en-

couraged me the year before in a play-writing workshop at E. R. Murrow High School in Brooklyn,
New York. When he called me up that summer and
told me that the play was being considered for the
Festival, I had forgotten all about it (honestly!). I
had been certain it couldn't be any good because the
writing itself had been so effortless and angst-free.
That winter, it was performed in a reading and I
met Michael Bennett, who directed it the following
spring. Some improvements in the script happened
during rehearsal, but the bulk of the play was identi-
cal to what I had scribbled the year before.

There's a valuable lesson here, I think, one that I
am constantly forgetting and that I will probably
have to keep relearning for the rest of my life: Stop
thinking about it and go for it!

Meet Glenwood High's fabulous four, the

SENIORS

Kit, Elaine, Alex, and Lori are very best friends. On the brink of graduation and adulthood, these popular seniors are discovering themselves, planning for the future, and falling in love. **Eileen Goudge $2.25 each**